Sleep problems

Yes

A. Have you had any problems with sleep?
   Difficulty falling asleep?................❏   Frequent or long periods of
   Restless or unrefreshing sleep? .....❏   being awake?...........................❏
   Early morning awakening..............❏

If YES to any of the above, continue below

1. Do you have any medical problems or physical pains? ....❏
2. Are you taking any medication? ....❏
3. Do any of the following apply?
   Drink alcohol, coffee, tea or eat before you sleep? ....❏
   Take day time naps? ....❏
   Experienced changes to your routine eg shift work? ....❏
   Disruptive noises during the night? ....❏
4. Do you have problems at least three times a week? ....❏
5. Has anyone told you that your snoring is loud and disruptive? ....❏
6. Do you get sudden uncontrollable sleep attacks during the day? ....❏
7. Low mood or loss of interest or pleasure? ....❏
8. Worried, anxious or tense? ....❏
9. How much alcohol do you drink in a typical week (number of standard
   drinks/week)? ....

Summing up

Positive to any of 1, 2 or 3:..❏
consider management of the underlying problem
Positive to 4: indication of **sleep problem** ....❏
Positive to 5: consider **sleep apnoea** ....❏
If positive to 6: consider **narcolepsy** ....❏
Positive to 7: consider **depression**...................................❏
Positive to 8: consider **anxiety** ....❏
If weekly drinking is more than 21 standard drinks for men and more than
14 for women, consider **alcohol use problems**.........................❏

Anxiety

Yes

A. Feeling tense or anxious? ....❏
B. Worrying a lot about things? ....❏

If YES to any of the above, continue below

1. Symptoms of arousal and anxiety? ....❏
2. Experienced intense or sudden fear unexpectedly or for no apparent reason?
   Fear of dying ....❏   Feeling dizzy,
   Fear of losing control ....❏   lighthearted or faint ....❏
   Pounding heart ....❏   Numbness or tingling
   Sweating........................❏   sensations....................❏
   Trembling or shaking.............❏   Feelings of unreality............❏
   Chest pains or   Nausea........................❏
      difficulty breathing...........❏
3. Experiences fear/anxiety in specific situations
   leaving familiar places ....❏
   travelling alone, e.g. train, car, plane ....❏
   crowds confined places/public places ....❏
4. Experienced fear/anxiety in social situations ....❏
   speaking in front of others ....❏
   social events ....❏
   eating in front of others ....❏
   worry a lot about what others think or self conciousness? ....❏

Summing up

Positive to A, B and 1, recurring regularly negative to 2, 3 and 4:
Indication of **generalized anxiety** ....❏
Positive to 1 and 2: indication of **panic disorder** ....❏
Positive to 1 and 3: indication of **agoraphobia** ....❏
Positive to 1 and 4: indication of **social phobia** ....❏

Functioning and disablement

A. During the past month, have you been limited in one or more of the following activities most of the time?

Self-care: bathing, dressing, eating? ....❏
Family relations: spouse, children, relatives? ....❏
Going to work or school? ....❏

Doing housework or household t...
Social activities, seeing friends? .
Remembering things? ....

Alcohol use problems

Yes

A. No. of units of alcohol in a typical day when drinking? . . . . ☐

B. No. of days/week having alcoholic drinks? . . . . ☐

If above limit, or if there is a regular / hazardous pattern, continue below

1. Have you been unable to stop, reduce or continue your drinking? . . . . ☐

2. Have you ever felt such a strong desire or urge to drink that you could
   not resist it? . . . . ☐

3. Did stopping or cutting down on your drinking ever cause you problems,
   such as:

   the shakes? . . . . ☐   heart beating fast? . . . . ☐
   being unable to sleep? . . . . ☐   headaches? . . . . ☐
   feeling nervous or restless? . . . . ☐   fits or seizures? . . . . ☐
   sweating? . . . . ☐

4. Have you ever continued to drink when you know that you had
   problems that can be made worse by drinking? . . . . ☐

5. Has anyone expressed concern about your drinking; for example,
   your family, friends or your doctor? . . . . ☐

Summing up

If A x B is 21/week or more for men, or 14/week or more for women:
possible **alcohol problem** . . . . ☐
If A x B is 21/week or more for men, or 14/week or more for women and positive
to any of 1–5:
likely **alcohol problem** . . . . ☐

B. Because ot these problems during the past month:

how many days were you unable to fully carry out your usual
daily activities? . . . .
how many days did you spend in bed in order to rest? . . . .

If there is more than one disorder present:

- best to treat an alcohol problem first, if present
- if low mood, treatment for depression takes priority over anxiety or unexplained somatic complaints
- if anxiety symptoms present, treatment for anxiety takes priority over unexplained somatic complaints. The latter increase in the presence of depression or anxiety.

If patient has an identified disorder:

- see relevant guideline to help determine treatment plan
- use relevant interactive summary card(s), if available, with the patient to help explain the disorder
- provide self help leaflets, if available, and explain how this should be used
- set up a follow-up visit(s) to review treatment.

If patient appears to have sub-threshold disorder(s):
(ie positive responses to many questions, but not enough to fulfil the diagnostic criteria for a disorder):

- medication may not be necessary
- use the relevant 'Advice and support to patient and family' section of the guidelines and provide patient leaflets, if available
- use relevant interactive summary card(s), if available, with the patient to help explain the disorder
- indicate that you are available for consultation should the need arise.

WHO Guide to Mental Health in Primary Care

Adapted for the UK, with permission, from *Diagnostic and Management Guidelines for Mental Disorders in Primary Care: ICD-10 Chapter V Primary Care Version*

The ROYAL
SOCIETY of
MEDICINE
PRESS Limited

*World Health Organization Collaborating
Centre for Research and Training for Mental Health*

WHO Guide to Mental Health in Primary Care

A guide to mental ill health in adults

Adapted for the UK, with permission, from *Diagnostic and Management Guidelines for Mental Disorders in Primary Care: ICD-10 Chapter V Primary Care Version*

Editorial Board:
David Goldberg, Linda Gask, Rachel Jenkins, Barry Lewis, Jo Paton, Debbie Sharp and André Tylee

Overall management of the project by:
Jo Paton under the direction of Professor Rachel Jenkins

The WHO Collaborating Centre for Research and Training for Mental Health gratefully acknowledges financial support towards development costs of the Guide from the NHS R&D programme. The Royal Society of Medicine gratefully acknowledges financial support for printing and distribution costs from PriMHE (Primary care Mental Health Education), Janssen-Cilag Ltd. and Pharmacia Corporation from unrestricted, educational grants.

UK Edition

World Health Organization Collaborating Centre for Research and Training for Mental Health

The ROYAL
SOCIETY *of*
MEDICINE
PRESS *Limited*

This edition published by the Royal Society of Medicine Press Ltd., 1 Wimpole Street, London W1G 0AE, UK

Website: http://www.rsm.ac.uk/

The authors have worked to ensure that all information in this book containing drug dosages, schedules and routes of administration is accurate at time of publication and consistent with standards set by the World Health Organization (WHO) and the general medical community. As medical research and practice advance, however, therapeutic standards may change. For this reason, and because human and mechanical errors sometimes occur, we recommend that readers follow the advice of a physician who is directly involved in their care or in the care of a member of their family.

Reference this book as: World Health Organization Collaborating Centre for Research and Training for Mental Health, eds. *WHO Guide to Mental Health in Primary Care*. London: Royal Society of Medicine Press, 2000.

British Library Cataloguing in Publication Data
A catalogue record is available for this book from the British Library

ISBN 1 85315 451 2

Phototypeset by Phoenix Photosetting, Chatham, Kent, UK
Printed in Great Britain by Ebenezer Baylis, The Trinity Press, Worcester, UK

Contents

Foreword   xi

Introduction   1

Prevalence of mental disorders   11

General referral criteria for mental disorders   12

Mental disorders   15

Acute psychotic disorders   15
Adjustment disorder (including acute stress reaction)   19
Alcohol misuse   22
Bereavement   28
Bipolar disorder   31
Chronic fatigue and chronic fatigue syndrome   35
Chronic mixed anxiety and depression   39
Chronic psychotic disorders   43
Delirium   48
Dementia   50
Depression   55
Dissociative (conversion) disorder   60
Drug use disorders   62
Eating disorders   67
Generalized anxiety   71
Panic disorder   75
Phobic disorders (includes agoraphobia and social phobia)   79
Post-traumatic stress disorder   82
Sexual disorders (female)   85
Sexual disorders (male)   88
Sleep problems (insomnia)   92
Unexplained somatic complaints   95

Learning disability   98

A guide to Mental Health Act assessments 103

England and Wales   103
Northern Ireland   107
Scotland   112

Template chart for local resources — statutory services   117

Template chart for local resources — voluntary agencies   119

Resource directory   120

Mental health in your practice: what does your practice provide?   136

Further reading and websites   138

What do different mental-health professionals do?   140

Psychological therapies: what are they?   143

Sources of primary mental healthcare training   146

References   152

Acknowledgements   168

Interactive summary cards — for discussion by professional and patient together   173

Alcohol problems   174
Anxiety   176
Chronic tiredness   178
Depression   180
Sleep problems   182
Unexplained somatic symptoms   184

Index   187

Contents of disks

Diagnostic and management summaries

Disk 1

Diagnostic check lists — for depression, anxiety, alcohol misuse, chronic fatigue, sleep problems and unexplained somatic symptoms

General referral criteria for mental disorders

Mental disorders
Acute psychotic disorders
Adjustment disorder (including acute stress reaction)
Alcohol misuse
Bereavement
Bipolar disorder
Chronic fatigue and Chronic fatigue syndrome
Chronic mixed anxiety and depression
Chronic psychotic disorders
Delirium
Dementia
Depression
Dissociative (conversion) disorder
Drug use disorders
Eating disorders
Generalized anxiety
Panic disorder
Phobic disorder
Post-traumatic stress disorder
Sexual disorders (female)
Sexual disorders (male)
Sleep problems (insomnia)
Unexplained somatic complaints

Learning disability

References

Interactive summary cards
Alcohol problems
Anxiety
Chronic tiredness

Depression
Sleep problems
Unexplained somatic complaints

Disk 2: Resources

For use with patients: information and self-help leaflets

Management strategies useful for a large number of disorders
01–1 Solving problems and achieving goals
01–2 Learning to relax
01–3 Coping with the side-effects of medication

Acute stress reaction
02 Psychological responses to traumatic stress: what to expect

Alcohol misuse
03–1 Responsible drinking guidelines
03–2 How to cut down on your drinking

Anxiety disorders
04–1 Anxiety and how to reduce it
     Controlled breathing exercises — for panic — page 8
04–2 Dealing with anxious thoughts
04–3 Overcoming particular fears (phobias)
04–4 Helping someone else overcome a phobia
04–5 Distinguishing between a panic attack and a heart attack

Bipolar disorder
05–1 What is bipolar disorder?
05–2 Lithium toxicity

Chronic tiredness
06–1 Chronic tiredness — for mild to moderate symptoms
06–2 Chronic Fatigue Syndrome — for more severe symptoms
06–3 Dealing with negative thinking in Chronic Fatigue
Syndrome

Depression
07–1 Depression: what is it? How is it treated? How to cope.
     Sources of help.
07–2 Activity planning
07–3 Dealing with depressive thinking
07–4 MAOI diet sheet
07–5 Ideas for enjoyable things to do

Drug misuse
08–1 Harm minimization advice
08–2 Sample drug-use diary

Eating disorders — bulimia
09–1 Food and behaviour diary
09–2 Monitoring and delaying binges

Psychosis
10–1 What to expect after an acute episode of psychosis
10–2 What is schizophrenia?
10–3 Coping with difficult behaviour
10–4 Early warning signs form

Sleep problems
11 Overcoming sleep problems

Unexplained physical complaints
12 Unexplained physical complaints

For use by professionals — checklists

13–1 CAGE questionnaire — screen for alcohol misuse
13–2 Audit questionnaire — screen for alcohol miuse
13–3 Abbreviated mental test score — screen for dementia
13–4 Social and living skills checklist — assess adequacy of care
      plan in chronic, severe illness

Connections between ICD-10 PHC and ICD-10 Chapter V

Resource directory

Mental health in your practice: what does your practice provide?

Foreword

In a general-practice surgery, every third or fourth patient seen has some form of mental disorder. Levels of disability among primary-care patients with such disorders are high: greater on average than disability among primary-care patients with common chronic diseases such as hypertension, diabetes, arthritis and back pain. Simple and effective treatments are available for many mental disorders and some can be treated more effectively than hypertension or coronary heart disease.

Changes in the way services are provided also emphasize the importance of primary care as a setting for mental healthcare. Over the past 30 years, the number of hospital beds available for people with mental illness has fallen, while the number of GPs and psychiatrists has risen. A direct result is that people in primary care need to work more closely with those in mental health services. Good mental healthcare is a collaborative effort. The Primary Care Team includes practice nurses, district nurses, health visitors, counsellors, clinical psychologists and school nurses, as well as GPs, all of whom may have a role in mental healthcare. The Community Mental Health Team may include nurses, occupational therapists, clinical psychologists, social workers and support workers, as well as psychiatrists. Families and friends, self-help and community groups also provide crucial support to people with a whole range of mental disorders: from transient distress to enduring psychotic illness. They need to talk to one another, respect each other's contribution and jointly agree who will provide which service to whom.

Despite this, mental-health provision has been dogged, perhaps more than any other area of healthcare, by differences in how we think about mental health and the words we use. This makes it hard for different professional groups and non-professionals to talk to each other. This handbook aims to ameliorate this problem. The diagnostic and management summaries it contains are based on the WHO International *Diagnostic and Management Guidelines for Mental Disorders in Primary Care* and are wholly compatible with ICD-10 Chapter V — which is the diagnostic framework used by psychiatric professionals. However, they have been simplified and extensively piloted to ensure that they are relevant to primary care. They also include management strategies based on a multi-axial approach — emphasizing the information needs of patients and their families, and simple social and psychological management strategies, in addition to medication.

This handbook is a resource that can be used in a number of ways. It can be used by an individual practitioner in the care of his or her patients. It can also be used by a primary-care team or a primary care organization (or local health group) to review, jointly with mental-health teams, the service they provide, identifying gaps and training needs or developing locally appropriate, shared criteria for referral to specialist services. We support this handbook and hope that its use improves communication and collaboration between all who have a stake in the provision of good primary mental healthcare.

Dr John Cox
President, Royal College of Psychiatrists

Claire Rayner
President, Patient's Association

Professor André Tylee
Director, Royal College of General Practitioners Unit for Mental Health Education in Primary Care

Christine Hancock
President, Royal College of Nursing

Introduction

Mental disorders are common and affect all of us at some time, if not ourselves directly then friends, family or work colleagues. Most people who suffer from mental disorders and who receive care from the health service do so in primary care, with the number of consultations for mental disorders second only to those for respiratory infections.[1] The numbers are very high[2] and, while most people suffer from mild conditions and recover quickly, a significant proportion suffer from chronic conditions[3] which cause moderate or high disability.[4] This book has been written to support primary-care professionals, primary care organizations and local health groups in this aspect of their work. It deals with conditions that are frequently seen in primary care and which can be managed effectively by general practitioners and their teams, supported as appropriate by secondary care. For each condition, a brief summary of how to diagnose and manage it is given. The management summaries include information for the patient, advice and support, descriptions of treatment methods and indications for specialist referrals. They are supported by a linked set of resources to help the General Practitioner (GP) or other clinician to carry out the management strategies recommended.

Resources provided

- **A mental disorder assessment guide.** This is to help the assessment of depression, anxiety, alcohol, sleep, chronic tiredness and unexplained somatic complaint disorders. To use it, start with the screening questions (in top boxes) to explore the presence of disorders and, if the disorder exists, you can continue below.
- **Interactive summary cards.** For the six disorders most common in primary care (depression, anxiety, alcohol problems, chronic fatigue, unexplained somatic complaints and sleep problems) two-page summaries have been produced. One page contains information for the practitioner; the other for the patient. With less information than the main summaries, but easier to see at a glance, they are meant to be used interactively. These are found on the disc, as well as on pages 174–185. They may be printed out and mounted on either side of a piece of A4 card and used

to facilitate discussion between practitioner and patient within a consultation.

• **A linked set of patient information and self-help leaflets** giving more information about the treatment and self-help strategies recommended. These are on the disc and can be printed out and given to patients to help reinforce the information that has been provided and also to encourage active participation in treatment. These vary in length and complexity. Some (for example, the one-page Problem-solving sheet) are suitable for use by General Practitioners in a consultation. Others (for example, the leaflet on Chronic Fatigue Syndrome) are more likely to be used by another member of the team, such as a counsellor, nurse or physiotherapist. The notation (R: x–x) 💾 appears in the text of a summary to indicate the existence of a linked resource leaflet.

Why were these disorders chosen?

The book contains a list of categories of mental disorders from the ICD-10 classification.

This is the result of a selection process that reflects:

• the public health importance of disorders (ie prevalence, morbidity or mortality, disability resulting from the condition, burdens imposed on the family or community, healthcare resources need)
• availability of effective and acceptable management (ie interventions with a high probability of benefit to the patient or his/her family are readily available within primary care and are acceptable to the patient and the community
• a reasonable consensus exists among primary-care practitioners and mental-health professionals regarding the diagnosis and management of the condition
• cross-cultural applicability (ie suggestions for identification and management are applicable in different cultural settings and healthcare systems)
• consistency with the main ICD-10 classification scheme (ie each diagnosis and diagnostic category corresponds to those in ICD-10)

All disorders included in this book are fairly common in primary-care settings and a management plan can be written for each of them.

The section for people with a learning disability has been separately identified because recognition and treatment of mental disorders present particular difficulties in this group and because mainstream adult mental-health services may not be appropriate for them. Learning disability is, of course, not itself a mental disorder.

How the diagnostic and management summaries were developed

The World Health Organization (WHO) developed a state-of-the-art classification of mental disorders for use in clinical practice and research. The *Tenth Revision of the International Classification of Diseases (ICD-10)* has many features that improve the diagnosis of mental disorders. To extend this development to primary-care settings, where most patients with mental disorders are seen, diagnostic and management guidelines were combined into the WHO book *Diagnostic and Management Guidelines for Mental Disorders in Primary Care (ICD-10 Chapter V, Primary Care Version)*. The guidelines were developed by an international group of GPs, family physicians, mental-health workers, public health experts, social workers, psychiatrists and psychologists with a special interest in mental health problems in primary care, using a consensus approach. The WHO guidelines were extensively field-tested in over 40 countries by 500 primary-care physicians to assess their relevance, ease of use and reliability. This work has been published.[5,6] Field trials using the WHO guidelines continue in various centres in the UK.

The diagnostic and management summaries in this handbook consist of the WHO's *International Diagnostic and Management Guidelines for Mental Disorders in Primary* Care, specially adapted (and up-dated) for use in Britain. They have been adapted in two stages. The first stage of adaptation to the UK setting was carried out in South Bristol by a panel of GPs and multidisciplinary representatives from community mental-health teams, using a consensus methodology. A randomized controlled trial of the handbook in 30 general practices in Bristol, measuring a range of mental-health outcomes, was then carried out.

The second stage of adaptation was carried out by a national, editorial team, coordinated by the WHO Collaborating Centre of the Institute of Psychiatry. The evidence base was reviewed (see below), information on psychological therapies was added, and information (on the Mental Health Act of England and Wales 1983, community resources and referral) was made appropriate to the whole of the UK. Representatives of primary-care nurses, counsellors and patient groups have made valuable suggestions to ensure that the information is accessible to these important groups. 3

Several rounds of consensus, including a conference, were held to debate the amendments and agree the final text. Names of those involved in this stage can be found in the Acknowledgements section.

The interactive handycards, the diagnostic checklist and most of the patient information leaflets were produced by the WHO's Division of Mental Health and Prevention of Substance Abuse, and endorsed by The Collegium Internationale Neuro-Psychopharmacologicum, the World Organization of National Colleges, Academies and Associations of General Practitioners and Family Physicians and the World Psychiatric Association. Some of the leaflets were developed by the WHO Collaborating Centre for Mental Health and Substance Abuse, as part of the Treatment Protocol Project.

The evidence on which the summaries are based

The diagnosis sections are based on the ICD-10 classification of mental disorders. ICD-10 is itself a consensus document, tested for reliability. The ICD-10 PHC diagnostic criteria presented here have been tested among primary-care professionals to check for validity and usefulness.

References supporting evidence have been given in line with the principles set out below:

a) Treatments (medication and psychotherapies)

The recommendations about medication are all in line with the British National Formulary (BNF). Where recommendations about medication are unexceptional and in line with both the BNF and established practice for many years, references have not been given.

References have been reserved for key statements about medication and about particular psychotherapies or for statements about which evidence and opinion are divided. It should be noted that most studies have been carried out in a secondary care setting. The mixed presentations of disorders found in primary care means that, generally speaking, both drugs and psychotherapies prove less efficacious, in comparison to placebo, in that setting than they do in more selected groups in secondary care. We have therefore included some discussion about what the evidence says, along with the references to the studies themselves. A grading of the quality of the evidence is also provided in the reference/notes section. Where possible, evidence has been given from Cochrane reviews, high-quality published reviews and meta-analyses or randomized controlled trials (RCTs). Discussions have been held with experts and authors of key areas of research.

The evidence has been graded as follows:

Strength of the evidence supporting the recommendation
A = Good evidence to support
B = Fair evidence to support
C = Preliminary evidence to support

Quality of the evidence supporting the statement
I = Evidence obtained from a meta-analysis of trials, including one or more well-designed RCTs
II = Evidence obtained from one well-designed RCT
III = Evidence obtained from one or more controlled trials, without randomization
IV = Evidence obtained from one or more uncontrolled studies
V = Opinions of respected authorities, based on clinical experience, descriptive studies or reports of expert committees. Occasionally the 'respected authorities' comprise collective patient experience. Where this is the case, it is clearly stated.

Where a qualitative review of previously published literature without a quantitative synthesis of the data is referenced, it has been graded in accordance with the type of studies the review includes.

Where a reference is marked 'N', this means that the notes contains additional information or a discussion of the issues, as well as the reference.

b) Information and advice
The sections on 'Essential information for patient and family' and 'Advice and support for patient and family' are primarily the result of consensus. There are no trials comparing the outcome of patients given different sorts of advice by their GP. The advice itself is based on a mixture of evidence and consensus of professionals and/or patients. A small number of references to supporting evidence have been given.

c) Referrals
The referral recommendations are based on consensus and will vary from place to place, depending on services available in all care sectors.

Connections to ICD-10 Chapter V
The ICD-10 PC Chapter V mental disorders classification, primary-care version, is a 'user friendly' version of the Tenth

Revision of the International Classification of Diseases (ICD-10) Chapter V. For practical reasons, the ICD-10 PC is a condensed version of ICD-10 Chapter V for easy application in busy primary-care settings. It has 23 categories instead of 457. It intends to cover the universe of mental disorders seen in primary-care settings in adults. As a classification, it is 'jointly exhaustive and mutually exclusive'. It may seem simplistic; however, it corresponds to the ICD-10 main volume. A chart that shows the grouping of the detailed specialty-adaptation categories into ICD-10 PC categories can be found on the disks.

How an individual practitioner might use the handbook

In the field trials, some practitioners used the summaries as a resource between consultations, to look something up. Others used the summaries interactively with the patient, to help explain the disorder and determine a treatment plan. The appropriate information and/or self-help leaflet can be printed out and given to the patient to reinforce what is said in the consultation. The interactive summary cards can be used to facilitate discussion between clinician and patient.

The text of the handbook, the leaflets and the interactive summary cards have been placed on disc as rich text format files. GPs or other team members, with regular access to a computer, could install the handbook on their computer, for ease of searching.

The handbook will also be a useful resource for educators of all generalist doctors and nurses.

Patients as partners

It is crucial for practitioners to decide on a management plan in partnership with the patient. This will help reduce the well-documented high level of 'non-compliance', where people do not take the medication prescribed for them. A partnership approach also lays stress on the patients' responsibility to help themselves. Many patients get better faster, or cope better with chronic illness, if they are actively involved in understanding what is happening to them and making changes to their lifestyle. Because the summaries are brief, they may appear prescriptive. Yet we hope that they can be used as a basis for discussion between the practitioner and patient about what is happening to them and why, which takes account of the patient's personal and cultural beliefs, and that they can together agree a plan of what to do.

Care programme approach

Where a patient is receiving care from mental-health services, they should have a Care Programme (comprising a written care plan reviewed regularly, and a named key worker who coordinates their care). There needs to be clear agreement about which elements of care are provided by the GP and which by the community team. Both team and patient need to know what the plan is in case of relapse, and have names and telephone numbers of the key people to contact easily to hand (eg the key worker identified on the front page of the notes). The summaries assume that these discussions will take place.

Needs of carers

People with chronic disorders are often cared for by friends or members of their family. The strain on these informal carers can be severe, resulting in an increased risk of both physical and mental ill health. It is important to review how the carer is managing and to encourage them to find ways of reducing the stress on them. Self-help groups, day care and respite care can all help. An assessment of the needs of the carer (under the Carer's Recognition and Services Act) can be requested from the local Social Services department. This advice is relevant to all chronic disorders and we have not repeated it on each individual summary.

Beyond diagnosis — a multi-axial approach

A short, diagnostic summary cannot capture the full clinical and social picture. The summaries focus on the diagnosis, severity and duration of the disorder, as an essential prerequisite of a specific management plan. The practitioner needs to add to this, as appropriate, assessing other factors such as social stresses linked to the symptoms, physical health, past and family history and the level of social support available from family and friends. Some of the management strategies outlined in the summaries and patient leaflets are easier for a patient who has good support from family or friends. Increased professional support could perhaps then be focused on those people who are more isolated.

Medication

Wherever possible, medication recommendations refer to a class of drug or a generic form. Where it is considered particularly useful or important, however, examples of particular, named drugs are given. **These are examples only and should not be**

7

taken as a WHO recommendation to prescribe that particular
brand. The summaries should be read in conjunction with the
British National Formulary, which contains information on every
individual drug.

How a practice team, primary care organization or local health group might use the handbook

Team working and training within primary care

The diagnostic and management summaries assume that the
resources available to primary-care teams will vary widely. The
'support to patient and family' can be offered by any member of
the primary-care team, who has suitable training and skills. GP,
nurse, health visitor, school nurse, practice counsellor and
psychologist may all contribute, and discussion to clarify the roles
of each is essential. It will be helpful to carry out an assessment of
the mental-health skills available within the team, in order to
make best use of the skills of all members and inform practice
training plans, as well as referral to external resources. This
assessment could be done by an individual practice, group of
practices or whole primary care organization. A list of sources of
training in primary mental healthcare and a checklist of ways a
practice can respond to the mental health needs of its patients is
provided on p. 146.

Team working between primary, secondary and social care

Primary care organizations could use the diagnostic and
management summaries as a basis to discuss and agree locally
appropriate referral criteria with specialist mental-health services.
It would be possible to work on a small number of disorders or to
work through all of them. This process might reveal gaps in local
services; for example, in the availability of structured
psychological therapies for affective disorders. Primary care
organizations may wish to consider ways of addressing these
gaps in their service development plans or in the commissioning
plans of Training Consortia.

Some primary care organizations or health groups might wish
to go further and address systems for communication between
primary and secondary care. Effective communication is a crucial
element of effective care, and misunderstandings between
primary care and mental-health services are very common.
Primary-care teams and community mental-health teams may

wish to meet to agree the roles, responsibilities and expectations of each member of both teams. A variety of different models have been tried, to improve communication as a whole and to improve the care of patients who are 'shared' between primary and secondary care in particular. Joint case registers of people with chronic mental illness is one of these. See the 'Further reading' section for sources of more information on this topic.

Information about resources in the community

The primary care organization or local health group might also produce a locally appropriate directory of services and community resources and distribute to its constituent practices. The information could be made available on computer or in a wall-chart format. Consideration will need to be given to regular up-dating of this information. Within each practice, the practice manager, or other team member, will need to consider how best to make the patient information leaflets available, how to obtain and insert the information about local services into the template wall charts and how best to make that information readily accessible to patients and all members of the practice team.

Localization

The diagnostic and management summaries are meant as a resource to local agencies. They will only be useful if they are actively disseminated — at practice, primary care organization and Health Authority levels. Local adaptation of the summaries to suit particular situations is welcomed and encouraged. To make it possible, we have included the text of the summaries in electronic format on a disc. Locally adapted pages can easily be inserted where required. A template to be filled in with information about local services is provided. While the diagnostic information is standard and used internationally, the management plan, particularly the referral criteria, will vary according to the availability of services locally and the training of healthcare workers.

The copyright for the diagnostic and management summaries rests with the World Health Organization. Where a primary care organization, local health group or Health Authority is producing locally adapted guidelines using the WHO summaries as a basis, we ask that you contact Professor Rachel Jenkins at the WHO Collaborating Centre Office, Institute of Psychiatry, De Crespigny Park, Denmark Hill, London SE5 8AF, UK. Tel: 020 7848 0383; E-mail: r.jenkins@iop.kcl.ac.uk

References

1 McCormick A, Fleming D, Charlton J. *Morbidity Statistics from General Practice: Fourth National Study 1991–1992*. London: HMSO, series MB5 no 3, 1995.

2 Ustun TB, Sartorius N. *Mental Illness in General Health Care: An International Study*. Chichester: John Wiley & Sons, 1995.

3 Mann A, Jenkins R, Besley E. The twelve month outcome of patients with neurotic illness in general practice. *Psychol Med* 11, 535–550, 1981.

4 Meltzer H, Gill B *et al*. *OPCS Survey of Psychiatric Morbidity in Great Britain Report 3: Economic Activity and Social Functioning of Adults With Psychiatric Disorders*. London: HMSO, 1995.

5 Goldberg D, Sharp D, Nanayakkara K. The field trial of the mental disorders section of ICD-10 designed for primary care (ICD10-PHC) in England. *Family Practice* 1995, 12(4).

6 Ustun B, Goldberg D, Cooper J, Simon G, Sartorius N: A new classification of menta disorders based on management for use in primary care (ICD10-PHC) *Br J Gen Pract* 1995, 45: 211–215.

Prevalence of mental disorders

Population and estimated general practice prevalence of mental disorder

Diagnosis	Weekly prevalence per 1000 adults aged 16–64	Number of patients aged 16–64 on GP list of 1800 (Assumes 63% of GP list is aged 16–64)
Mixed anxiety and depression	77	87
Generalized anxiety	31	36
Depressive episode	21	24
All phobias	11	13
Obsessive compulsive disorder	12	14
Panic disorder	8	9
All neuroses	160	182
Functional psychoses	4.4	5

Source: OPCS Survey of Psychiatric Morbidity Report 1. London: HMSO, 1995.

Variations in prevalence of mental disorders in adults aged 16–64 living in private households in Great Britain between rural and urban areas in the UK

Disorder Prevalence per 1000 adults		Urban	Semi-rural	Rural
Neuroses	Women	216	156	150
	Men	133	117	78
Psychoses	Women	5	5	1
	Men	6	5	3

Source: OPCS Survey of Psychiatric Morbidity, Report 1. London: HMSO, 1995.

General referral criteria for mental disorders

A main objective of the *WHO Guide to Mental Health in Primary Care* is to extend the expertise of the primary-care clinician and improve the cooperation and communication between primary care and secondary mental-health services. With this understanding, the following guidelines have been prepared.

Referral to secondary mental-health services should be considered in the following circumstances:

- if the patient is displaying signs of suicidal intent or if there seems to be a risk of harm to others
- if the patient is so disabled by their mental disorder that they are unable to leave their home, look after their children or fulfil other activities of daily living
- if the GP requires the expertise of secondary care to confirm a diagnosis or implement specialist treatment
- if the GP feels that the therapeutic relationship with the patient has broken down
- if primary care interventions and voluntary/non-statutory options have been exhausted
- if there is severe physical deterioration of the patient
- if particular psychotropic medication is required eg clozapine, lithium or donezepil
- if the patient requests a referral.

When making a referral to secondary mental-health services, social services or voluntary/non-statutory organizations, the GP should:

- have access to a local resource directory
- consider coordination issues around the referral (eg care programme approach, key worker)
- consider implications for the continuing care of the physical health of the patient.

All referral criteria constitute part of the guideline for that particular disorder and assume that, as far as possible, the guideline for diagnosis and management has been followed.

It is helpful if referral letters include as many as possible of the following:

- The patient's name, hospital number (if known), date of birth, address and telephone number
- The presenting complaint
- The reason for referral, including whether for advice only for GP to manage, or for psychiatrist to manage
- Past psychiatric history
- Background
- Current mental state
- Current medication, details of any medication tried in the past few weeks
- Drugs and alcohol history
- Details of carers and significant others.

Key to signs used in the main text:

💾 R: 1-1	A resource relevant to the point in the text may be found on the disk — usually a patient information and self-help leaflet or a diagnostic questionnaire. (R = resource. The number refers to the number of the leaflet or questionnaire.)
N2	The reference section contains further information about the point made in the text. (N = further information. The number refers to the number of the reference.)
F23	This is the code in ICD-10 PC Chapter V (ie the International Classification of Diseases, primary care version, mental health chapter. A full list of how the primary-care codes relate to the codes from the main ICD-10 volume can be found on disk 2.

The '#' code is used in ICD-10 PC Chapter V only. It refers to 'condensed' codes. For example, 'F00# — Dementia' refers to all different types of dementia listed in F00–F03 and their related fourth and fifth character codes.

Reference numbers.
A grading of the evidence can be found in the reference section. The evidence has been graded as described in the Introduction.

Acute psychotic disorders — F23

Includes: *acute schizophrenia-like psychosis, acute delusional psychosis, and other acute and transient psychotic disorders*

Presenting complaints

Patients may experience:

- hallucinations, eg hearing voices when no one is around
- strange beliefs or fears
- apprehension, confusion
- perceptual disturbances.

Families may ask for help with behaviour changes that cannot be explained, including strange or frightening behaviour (eg withdrawal, suspiciousness, threats).

Young adults may present with persistent changes in functioning, behaviour or personality (eg withdrawal) but without florid psychotic symptoms.[N1]

Diagnostic features

Recent onset of:

- hallucinations (false or imagined sensations, eg hearing voices when no one is around).
- delusions (firmly held ideas that are often false and not shared by others in the patient's social, cultural or ethnic group, eg patients believe they are being poisoned by neighbours, receiving messages from television, or being looked at by others in some special way).
- disorganized or strange speech
- agitation or bizarre behaviour
- extreme and labile emotional states.

Differential diagnosis

- Physical disorders that can cause psychotic symptoms include:
  — drug induced psychosis
  — alcoholic hallucinosis
  — infectious or febrile illness
  — epilepsy
Refer to 'Delirium — FO5' for other potential causes.
- 'Chronic psychotic disorders — F20#', if psychotic symptoms are recurrent or chronic.

15

A

- **'Bipolar disorder — F31'**,, if symptoms of mania (eg elevated mood, racing speech or thoughts, exaggerated self-worth) are prominent.
- **'Depression** (depressive psychosis) **— F32#'**, if depressive delusions are prominent.

Essential information for patient and family

- Agitation and strange behaviour can be symptoms of a mental illness.
- Acute episodes often have a good prognosis,[N2] but long-term course of the illness is difficult to predict from an acute episode.
- Advise patient and family about the importance of medication, how it works and possible side-effects. (R: 1–3)🖫
- Continued treatment may be needed for several months after symptoms resolve.

If the patient requires treatment under the Mental Health Act, advise family about related legal issues (see the guides to the Mental Health Acts, pages 103–118).

Advice and support of patient and family (R: 10-1) 🖫

- Ensure the safety of the patient and those caring for him/her:
  — family or friends should be available for the patient if possible
  — ensure that the patient's basic needs (eg food and drink and accommodation) are met.
- Minimize stress and stimulation.
- Do not argue with psychotic thinking (you may disagree with the patient's beliefs, but do not try to argue that they are wrong).
- Avoid confrontation or criticism, unless it is necessary to prevent harmful or disruptive behaviour.[N3]
- If there is a significant risk of suicide, violence or neglect, admission to hospital or close observation in a secure place may be required. If the patient refuses treatment, legal measures may be needed.
- Assess ability to drive safely. Inform DVLA as appropriate, and in all cases where the patient is a heavy goods vehicle or PSV driver.[N4]
- Encourage resumption of normal activities after symptoms improve.

Referral

Referral should be made under the following conditions:

- as an emergency, if the risk of suicide, violence or neglect is considered significant

- urgently for ALL first episodes, to confirm the diagnosis and arrange care planning and appointment of key worker. A home visit may be required. Specific interventions for people experiencing their first episode of psychosis, including specific psycho-education of the patient and family, may be available[5]
- for ALL relapses, to review the effectiveness of the care plan, unless there is an established previous response to treatment and it is safe to manage the patient at home
- if there is non-compliance with treatment, problematic side-effects, failure of community treatment, or concerns about co-morbid drug and alcohol misuse.

Particularly on relapse, referral may be to the Community Mental Health Team or to a member of it, such as a community psychiatric nurse, as well as to a psychiatrist.

If there is fever, rigidity and/or labile blood pressure, stop antipsychotic medication and refer immediately to the on-call physician for investigation of neuroleptic malignant syndrome.

Medication

- Antipsychotic medication can reduce psychotic symptoms over 10–14 days. Where access to a specialist is speedy and symptoms relatively mild, especially for a first referral, the specialist may prefer to see the patient unmedicated.
- Examples of drugs you may wish to use before the patient sees a specialist include an atypical antipsychotic[N6] (eg olanzapine, 5–10 mg a day, or risperidone, 4–6 mg per day) or a typical drug, eg haloperidol (1.5–4 mg up to three times a day) (see BNF section 4.2.1). Patients experiencing a first episode of psychosis require lower doses of medication and may benefit from an atypical drug.[N7] In a case of relapse where the patient has previously responded to a drug, restart that drug. The dose should be the lowest possible for the relief of symptoms.[8]
- Anti-anxiety medication may also be used for the short term in conjuction with neuroleptics to control acute agitation (see BNF section 4.1.2). (Examples include diazepam [5–10 mg up to four times a day] or lorazepam [1–2 mg up to four times a day].) If required, diazepam can be given rectally, or lorazepam IM (though this must be kept refrigerated).
- Continue antipsychotic medication for at least six months after symptoms resolve.[9] Close supervision is usually needed in order to encourage patient agreement.
- Be alert to the risk of co-morbid use of street drugs (eg amphetamines) and alcohol.

17

- Monitor for side-effects of medication:
  — Acute dystonias or spasms may be managed with oral or injectable antiparkinsonian drugs (see BNF section 4.9.2) (eg procyclidine [5 mg three times per day] or orphenadrine [50 mg three times per day]).
  — Parkinsonian symptoms (eg tremor, akinesia) may be managed with oral antiparkinsonian drugs (see BNF section 4.9.2) (eg procyclidine [5 mg three times per day] or orphenadrine [50 mg three times per day]).
  Withdrawal of antiparkinsonian drugs should be attempted after two to three months without symptoms, as these drugs are liable to misuse and may impair memory.
  — Akathisia (severe motor restlessness) may be managed with dosage reduction or beta-blockers (for example, with propranolol [30–80 mg a day]) (see BNF section 2.4). Switching to a low-potency antipsychotic (eg olanzapine or quetiapine) may help.
  — Other side-effects, eg weight gain and sexual dysfuction.

More detail on anti-psychotic drugs and their differing side effect profiles can be found in the *Maudsley Prescribing Guidelines*.[10]

Resources for patients and families
Resource leaflets: 1–3 *Coping with the side-effects of medication* and 10–1 *What to expect after an acute episode of psychosis*.

MINDinfoLINE   0345 660163
(National telephone information service on mental health Issues)

SANEline   0345 678000 (seven nights, 2 pm–midnight)
(National helpline for mental health information and support to anyone coping with mental illness)

Manic Depression Fellowship   020 8974 6550
(Support and information for people with manic depression and their families and friends)

National Schizophrenia Fellowship advice line
020 8974 6814 (Monday–Friday, 10.30 am–3 pm)
(Advice and information for people suffering from schizophrenia, their families and carers).

Adjustment disorder — F43.2 (including acute stress reaction)

Presenting complaints
- Patients feel overwhelmed or unable to cope.
- There may be stress-related physical symptoms such as insomnia, headache, abdominal pain, chest pain and palpitations
- Patients may report symptoms of acute anxiety or depression
- Alcohol use may increase.

Diagnostic features
- Acute reaction to a recent stressful or traumatic event.
- Extreme distress resulting from a recent event, or preoccupation with the event.
- Symptoms may be primarily somatic.
- Other symptoms may include:
  — low or sad mood
  — anxiety
  — worry
  — feeling unable to cope.

Acute reaction usually lasts from a few days to several weeks.

Differential diagnosis
Acute symptoms may persist or evolve over time. If significant symptoms persist longer than one month, consider an alternative diagnosis.

- If significant symptoms of depression persist, see 'Depression — F32#'.
- If significant symptoms of anxiety persist, see 'Generalized anxiety — F41.1'.
- If significant symptoms of both depression and anxiety persist, see 'Chronic mixed anxiety and depression — F41.2'.
- If stress-related somatic symptoms persist, see 'Unexplained somatic complaints — F45'.
- If symptoms are due to a loss, see 'Bereavement — Z63'.
- If anxiety is long-lasting and focused on memories of a previous traumatic event, see 'Post-traumatic stress disorder — F43.1'.

19

If dissociative symptoms (sudden onset of unusual or dramatic somatic symptoms) are present, see **'Dissociative (conversion) disorder — F44'**.

Essential information for patient and family

- Stressful events often have mental and physical effects. The acute state is a natural reaction to events. (R: 2)🖳
- Stress-related symptoms usually last only a few days or weeks.

Advice and support of patient and family[N11]

- Review and reinforce positive steps the patient has taken to deal with the stress.
- Identify steps the patient can take to modify the situation that produced the stress. 🖳 If the situation cannot be changed, discuss coping strategies. (R: 1–1)
- Identify relatives, friends and community resources able to offer support.
- Encourage a return to usual activities within a few weeks.
- Short-term rest and relief from stress may help the patient. Consider short-term sickness certification.
- Encourage the patient to acknowledge the personal significance of the stressful event.
- Offering a further consultation with a member of the primary-care team, to see how the situation develops, can be valuable in helping the patient through the episode.

Medication

Most acute stress reactions will resolve without the use of medication. Skilled GP advice and reassurance is as effective as benzodiazepines.[N12] If severe anxiety symptoms occur, however, consider using anti-anxiety drugs for up to three days. If the patient has severe insomnia, use hypnotic drugs for up to three days. Doses should be as low as possible. (See BNF sections 4.1.1 and 4.1.2)

Referral

See general referral criteria. Usually self-limiting.

Routine referral to secondary mental health services is advised if:

- symptoms persist and general referral criteria are met
- unsure of the diagnosis

Consider recommending a practice counsellor or voluntary/non-statutory counselling[13] services in all other cases where symptoms persist.

Resources for patients and families

Resource leaflets: 1–1 *Problem solving* and 2 *What to expect after traumatic stress*.

UK Register of Counsellors   01788 568739
(Provides names and addresses of British Association of Counsellors [BAC]-accredited counsellors)

Samaritans   See local telephone directory
(Support by listening for those feeling lonely, despairing or suicidal)

Victim Support Supportline   0845 30 30 900 (9 am–9 pm, Monday–Friday; 9 am–7 pm, Saturday and Sunday; 9 am–5 pm, Bank holidays)
(Emotional and practical support for victims of crime)

Childline   0800 1111
(Freephone 24-hour helpline for children and young people in trouble or danger)

Citizens Advice Bureau   See local telephone directory
(Free advice and information on social security benefits, housing, family and personal matters, money advice and other issues)

Relate   01788 573 241
(Counselling and psychosexual therapy for adults with relationship difficulties).

Alcohol misuse — F10

Presenting complaints

Patients may present with:

- depressed mood
- nervousness
- insomnia
- physical complications of alcohol use (eg ulcer, gastritis, liver disease, hypertension)
- accidents or injuries due to alcohol use
- poor memory or concentration
- evidence of self-neglect (eg poor hygiene)
- failed treatment for depression.

There may also be:

- legal and social problems due to alcohol use (eg marital problems, domestic violence, child abuse or neglect, missed work)
- signs of alcohol withdrawal (sweating, tremors, morning sickness, hallucinations, seizures).

Patients may sometimes deny or be unaware of alcohol problems. Family members may request help before patient does (eg because patient is irritable at home or missing work). Problems may also be identified during routine health promotion screening.

Diagnostic features

- Harmful alcohol use:
  - heavy alcohol use (eg over 28 units per week for men, over 21 units per week for women)
  - overuse of alcohol has caused physical harm (eg liver disease, gastrointestinal bleeding), psychological harm (eg depression or anxiety due to alcohol), or has led to harmful social consequences (eg loss of job).
- Alcohol dependence. Dependence is present when three or more of the following are present:
  - Strong desire or compulsion to use alcohol
  - difficulty controlling alcohol use
  - withdrawal (anxiety, tremors, sweating) when drinking is ceased

- tolerance (eg drinks large amounts of alcohol without appearing intoxicated)
- continued alcohol use despite harmful consequences.

Blood tests such as gamma glutamyl transferase (GGT) and mean corpuscular volume (MCV) can help identify heavy drinkers. Administering the CAGE (R: 13–1) 🖫 or AUDIT (R: 13–2) 🖫 questionnaire may also help diagnosis.

Differential diagnosis

Reducing alcohol use may be desirable for some patients who do not fit the above guidelines.

Symptoms of anxiety or depression may occur with heavy alcohol use. Alcohol use can also mask other disorders, eg agoraphobia, social phobia and generalized anxiety disorder. Assess and manage symptoms of depression or anxiety if symptoms continue after a period of abstinence. See '**Depression — F32#**' or '**Generalized Anxiety — F41.1**'.

Drug misuse may also co-exist with this condition.

Essential information for patient and family

- Alcohol dependence is an illness with serious consequences.
- Ceasing or reducing alcohol use will bring mental and physical benefits.
- Drinking during pregnancy may harm the baby.
- For most patients with alcohol dependence, physical complications of alcohol abuse or psychiatric disorder, abstinence from alcohol is the preferred goal.[14] Sometimes, abstinence is also necessary for social crises, to regain control over drinking or because of failed attempts at reducing drinking. Because abrupt abstinence can cause withdrawal symptoms, medical supervision is necessary.
- In some cases of harmful alcohol use without dependence, or where the patient is unwilling to quit, controlled or reduced drinking is a reasonable goal.
- Relapses are common. Controlling or ceasing drinking often requires several attempts. Outcome depends on the motivation and confidence of the patient.

Advice and support to patient and family[15]

- For all patients:
  — Discuss costs and benefits of drinking from the patient's perspective.
  — Feedback information about health risks, including the results of GGT and MCV.

— Emphasize personal responsibility for change.
— Give clear advice to change.
— Assess and manage physical health problems and nutritional deficiencies (eg vitamin B).
— Consider options for problem-solving (R: 1–1) 📖 or targeted counselling to deal with life problems related to alcohol use.

• If there is no evidence of physical harm due to drinking, or if the patient is unwilling to quit, a controlled drinking programme is a reasonable goal:
— Negotiate a clear goal for decreased use (eg no more than two drinks per day with two alcohol-free days per week).
— Discuss strategies to avoid or cope with high-risk situations (eg social situations, stressful events).
— Introduce self-monitoring procedures (eg a drinking diary) and safer drinking behaviours (eg time restrictions, drinking more slowly). (R: 3–2) 📖

• For patients with physical illness and/or dependency, or failed attempts at controlled drinking, an abstinence programme is indicated.

• For patients willing to stop now:
— Set a definite day to quit.
— Discuss symptoms and management of alcohol withdrawal.
— Discuss strategies to avoid or cope with high-risk situations (eg social situations, stressful events).
— Make specific plans to avoid drinking (eg ways to face stressful events without alcohol, ways to respond to friends who still drink).
— Help patients to identify family members or friends who will support ceasing alcohol use.
— Consider options for support after withdrawal.

• For patients not willing to stop or reduce now, a harm reduction programme is indicated:
— Do not reject or blame.
— Clearly point out medical and social problems caused by alcohol.
— Consider thiamine preparations.
— Make a future appointment to re-assess health and alcohol use.

• For patients who do not succeed, or relapse:
— Identify and give credit for any success.
— Discuss the situations that led to relapse.
— Return to earlier steps above.

Self-help organizations (eg Alcoholics Anonymous), voluntary and non-statutory agencies are often helpful.[16]

Medication

- For patients with mild withdrawal symptoms, frequent monitoring, support, reassurance, adequate hydration and nutrition are sufficient treatment without medication.[17]
- Patients with a moderate withdrawal syndrome require benzodiazepines *in addition*. Most can be detoxified, with a good outcome, as outpatients or at home.[18] Community detoxification should only be undertaken by practitioners with appropriate training and supervision.
- Patients at risk of a complicated withdrawal syndrome (eg with a history of fits or delirium tremens, very heavy use and high tolerance, significant polydrug use, severe comorbid medical or psychiatric disorder) who lack social support or are a significant suicide risk require inpatient detoxification.
- Chlordiazepoxide (Librium) at 10 mg, is recommended. The initial dose should be titrated against withdrawal symtoms, within a range of 5–40 mg four times a day. (See BNF section 4.10.) This requires close, skilled supervision.
- The following regime is commonly used, although the dose level and length of treatment will depend on the severity of alcohol dependence and individual patient factors (eg weight, sex and liver function):
  Day 1 and 2:   20–30 mg QDS
  Day 3 and 4:   15 mg QDS
  Day 5:   10 mg QDS
  Day 6:   10 mg BD
  Day 7:   10 mg nocte
- Chlormethiazole is not recommended for craving or detoxification under any circumstances.[19]
- Dispensing should be daily or involve the support of family members to prevent the risk of misuse or overdose. Confirm abstinence by checking the breath for alcohol, or using a saliva test or breathalyser for the first three to five days.
- Thiamine (150 mg per day in divided doses) should be given orally for one month.[20] As oral thiamine is poorly absorbed, transfer patient immediately to a clinic with appropriate resuscitation facilities for parenteral supplementation if any *one* of the following is present: ataxia, confusion, memory disturbance, delirium tremens, hypothermia and hypotension, opthalmoplegia or unconsciousness.
- Daily supervision is essential in the first few days, then

25

advisable thereafter, to adjust dose of medication, assess whether the patient has returned to drinking, check for serious withdrawal symptoms and maintain support.

- Anxiety and depression often co-occur with alcohol misuse. The patient may have been using alcohol to self-medicate. If symptoms of anxiety or depression increase or remain after a period of abstinence of more than a month, see '**Depression — F32#**' and '**Generalized Anxiety — F41.1**'. Selective serotonin re-uptake inhibitor (SSRI) anti-depressants are preferred to tricyclics because of the risk of tricyclic–alcohol interactions (fluoxetine, paroxetine and citalopram do not interact with alcohol.) (See BNF section 4.3.3.) For anxiety, benzodiazepines should be avoided because of their high potential for abuse.[21] (See BNF section 4.1.2.)

- Acamprosate may help to maintain abstinence from alcohol in some cases, but routine use is not currently recommended.

For further information on alcohol detoxification, see *Drug Misuse and Dependence — Guidelines on Clinical Management.*[22]

For information on brief interventions for people whose drinking behaviour puts them at risk of becoming dependent, see Alcohol Concern's *Brief Intervention Guidelines.*[23]

Referral

Consider referral:

- to non-statutory Alcohol Advice and Counselling Agency (if available), and if no psychiatric illness is present
- to a specialist NHS alcohol service if the patient has alcohol dependence and requires an abstinence-based group programme or has an associated psychiatric disorder, or if there are no appropriately trained practitioners available in primary care
- for general hospital inpatient detoxification if the patient does not meet the criteria for community detoxification (see above)
- to targeted counselling, if available, to deal with the social consequences of drinking (eg relationship counselling)
- non-urgently to secondary mental health services if there is a severe mental illness (see relevant disorder), or if symptoms of mental illness persist after detoxification and abstinence.

If available, specific, social skills training[N24] and community-based treatment packages[N25] both may be effective in reducing drinking.

Resources for patients and families

Resource leaflets: 1–1 *Problem-solving* 3–1 *Responsible drinking guidelines* and 3–2 *How to cut down on your drinking.*

Al — Anon Family Groups UK and Eire   020 7403 0888
(24-hr helpline)
(Understanding and support for families and friends of alcoholics whether still drinking or not)

Alateen
(For young people aged 12–20 affected by others' drinking)

Alcoholics Anonymous   0700 0780977 (24-hr helpline)
(Helpline and support groups for men and women trying to achieve and maintain sobriety and help other alcoholics to get sober)

Drinkline National Alcohol Helpline   0345 320202
(UK-wide; charges at local rates)

Secular Organisations for Sobriety (SOS)   0700 78 1230
(A non-religious self-help group)

Northern Ireland Community Addiction Service
02890 664 434

Scottish Council on Alcohol   0143 338677

Health Education Authority   020 7222 5300

Health Education Board for Scotland   0131 536 5500
(Provide leaflets to support brief interventions for people at risk of becoming dependent on alcohol).

Bereavement — Z63

Presenting complaints

An acute grief reaction is a normal, understandable reaction to loss.

The patient:

- feels overwhelmed by loss
- is preoccupied with the lost loved one
- may present with somatic symptoms following loss.

Grief may be experienced on loss of a loved one and also other significant losses (eg loss of job, lifestyle, limb, breakdown of relationship). It may precipitate or exacerbate other psychiatric conditions, and may be complicated, delayed or incomplete, leading to seemingly unrelated problems years after the loss.

Diagnostic features

Normal grief includes preoccupation with loss of loved one. However, this may be accompanied by symptoms resembling depression, such as:

- low or sad mood
- disturbed sleep
- loss of interest
- guilt or self-criticism
- restlessness
- guilt about actions not taken by the person before the death of the loved one
- seeing the deceased person or hearing their voice
- thoughts of joining the deceased.

The patient may:

- withdraw from usual activities and social contacts
- find it difficult to think of the future
- increase use of drugs or alcohol.

Differential diagnosis

- 'Depression — F32#'.

Bereavement is a process. A helpful model is to think of four tasks to be completed by the bereaved person:

— accepting the reality of the loss — the patient may feel numb
— experiencing the pain of grief
— adapting to the world without the deceased
— 'letting go' of the deceased and moving on.

Consider depression if:

- the person becomes stuck at any point in the process
- a full picture of depression is still present two months after the loss
- there are signs that the grief is becoming abnormal (severe depressive symptoms of retardation, guilt, feelings of worthlessness, hopelessness or suicidal ideation of a severity or duration that significantly interferes with daily living).

There is a higher risk of an abnormal grief reaction where the bereaved person is socially isolated or has a history or depression or anxiety; where the relationship between the bereaved and the dead person was ambivalent; where the dead person was a child; and where the death was violent, occurred by suicide or occurred suddenly in traumatic circumstances (especially if the body is not present).

Essential information for patient and family

- Important losses are often followed by intense sadness, crying, anger, disbelief, anxiety, guilt or irritability.
- Bereavement typically includes preoccupation with the deceased (including hearing or seeing the person).
- A desire to discuss the loss is normal.
- Inform patients, especially those at greater risk of developing an abnormal grief reaction, of local agencies, such as Cruse Bereavement Care, which offer bereavement counselling and aim to help guide people through their normal grief.[26]

Advice and support to patient and family

- Enable the bereaved person to talk about the deceased and the circumstances of the death.
- Encourage free expression of feelings about the loss (including feelings of sadness, guilt or anger).
- Offer reassurance that recovery will take time. Some reduction in burdens (eg work or social commitments) may be necessary.
- Explain that intense grieving will fade slowly over several months but that reminders of the loss may continue to provoke feelings of loss and sadness.
- Take into account the cultural context of the loss.[27]

Medication

Avoid medication if possible. If the grief reaction becomes abnormal (see 'Differential diagnosis' above), see '**Depression — F32#**' for advice on the use of antidepressants.

Disturbed sleep is to be expected. If severe insomnia occurs, short-term use of hypnotic drugs may be helpful but use should be limited to two weeks. (See BNF section 4.1.1.) Avoid the use of anxiolytics.

Referral

Recommend voluntary organisations, eg CRUSE, for support through a normal grieving process.

Referral to secondary mental health services is advised:

• if the patient is severely depressed or showing psychotic features (see relevant disorder)
• non-urgently, if symptoms have not resolved by one year despite bereavement counselling.

Consider practice counsellor or non-statutory bereavement counsellors[13] in all other cases where symptoms persist.

Bereaved children may benefit from family counselling through the Child and Family Psychiatry service.

Refer bereaved people with learning disabilities to specialist disability team or specialist learning disability counsellor.

Resources for patients and their families

Cruse Bereavement Care   020 8332 7227 (helpline)
(One-to-one bereavement counselling, self-referral preferred)

Compassionate Friends   0117 953 9639 (helpline)
(Befriending and support for bereaved parents, grandparents, siblings)

Still Birth and Neonatal Death Society (SANDS)
020 7436 5881
(Information, emotional and physical support to parents who have lost a baby)

Foundation for the Study of Infant Deaths (FSID)
020 7235 1721 (24-hr)

Papyrus   01706 214449
(Self-help for parents of young people who have committed suicide)
c/o The Administration, Rosendale GH, Union Road, Rawtenstall, Rosendale, Lancs, BB4 6NE.

Bipolar disorder — F31

Presenting complaints

Patients may have a period of depression, mania or excitement with the pattern described below.

Referral may be made by others due to lack of insight.

Diagnostic features

- Periods of mania with:
  - increased energy and activity
  - elevated mood or irritability
  - rapid speech
  - loss of inhibitions
  - decreased need for sleep
  - increased importance of self.
- The patient may be easily distracted.
- The patient may also have periods of depression with:
  - low or sad mood
  - loss of interest or pleasure.
- The following associated symptoms are frequently present:
  - disturbed sleep
  - guilt or low self-worth
  - fatigue or loss of energy
  - poor concentration
  - disturbed appetite
  - suicidal thoughts or acts.

Either type of episode may predominate. Episodes may alternate frequently or may be separated by periods of normal mood. In severe cases, patients may have hallucinations (hearing voices or seeing visions) or delusions (strange or illogical beliefs) during periods of mania or depression.

Differential diagnosis

- 'Alcohol misuse — F10' or 'Drug use disorder — F11#' can cause similar symptoms.

Essential information for patient and family

- Unexplained changes in mood and behaviour can be symptoms of an illness.
- Effective treatments are available. Long-term treatment can prevent future episodes.

- If left untreated, manic episodes may become disruptive or dangerous. Manic episodes often lead to loss of job, legal problems, financial problems or high-risk sexual behaviour. When the first, milder symptoms of mania or hypomania occur, referral is often indicated and the patient should be encouraged to see their GP straight away.
- Inform patients who are on lithium of the signs of lithium toxicity (see 'Medication' below). (R: 5–2) 💾

Advice and support to patient and family (R: 5–1) 💾

- During depression, assess risk of suicide. (Has the patient frequently thought of death or dying? Does the patient have a specific suicide plan? Has he/she made serious suicide attempts in the past? Can the patient be sure not to act on suicidal ideas?) Close supervision by family or friends may be needed. Ask about risk of harm to others. (See **'Depression — F32#'**).
- During manic periods:
  — avoid confrontation unless necessary to prevent harmful or dangerous acts
  — advise caution regarding impulsive or dangerous behaviour
  — close observation by family members is often needed
  — if agitation or disruptive behaviour are severe, hospitalization may be required.
- During depressed periods, consult management guidelines for depression (See **'Depression — F32#'**).
- Describe the illness and possible future treatments.
- Encourage the family to consult, even if the patient is reluctant.
- Work with patient and family to identify early warning symptoms of mood swings, in order to avoid major relapse.
- For patients able to identify early symptoms of a forthcoming 'high', advise:
  — ceasing consumption of tea, coffee and other caffeine-based stimulants
  — avoiding stimulating or stressful situations (eg parties)
  — planning for a good night's sleep
  — taking relaxing exercise during the day, eg swimming or a walk before bed
  — avoiding making major decisions
  — taking steps to limit capacity to spend money (eg give credit cards to a friend).[28]
- Assess ability to drive safely. Inform DVLA as appropriate and in all cases where the patient is an HGV or PSV driver.[N4]

Medication

32

- If the patient displays agitation, excitement or disruptive behaviour, antipsychotic medication may be needed initially[29] (see BNF section 4.2.) (eg haloperidol [1.5–4 mg up to three times a day]). The doses should be the lowest possible for the relief of symptoms,[30] although some patients may require higher doses. If antipsychotic medication causes acute dystonic reactions (muscle spasms) or marked extrapyramidal symptoms (eg stiffness or tremors), antiparkinsonian medication (eg procyclidine [5 mg orally up to three times a day]) may be helpful. (See BNF section 4.9.) Routine use is not necessary.

- Benzodiazepines may also be used in the short term in conjunction with antipsychotic medication to control acute agitation.[31] (See BNF section 4.1.2.) Examples include diazepam (5–10 mg up to four times a day) or lorazepam (1–2 mg up to four times a day). If required, diazepam can be given rectally, or lorazepam IM (although it must be kept refrigerated).

- Lithium can help relieve mania[32] and depression[33] and can prevent episodes from recurring.[34] One usually commences or stops taking lithium only with specialist advice. Some GPs are confident about restarting lithium treatment after a relapse. Alternative mood-stabilizing medications include carbamazepine and sodium valproate. If used in the acute phase, lithium takes several days to show effects.

   If lithium is prescribed:
— There should be a clear agreement between the referring GP and the specialist as to who is monitoring lithium treatment. Lithium monitoring is ideally carried out using an agreed protocol. If carried out in primary care, monitoring should be done by a suitably trained person.
— Levels of lithium in the blood should be measured frequently when adjusting the dose, and every three months in stable patients, 10–14 hours post-dose (desired blood level is 0.4–0.8 mmol/L).[N35] **If blood levels are more than 1.5 mmol/L, or there is diarrhoea and vomiting, stop the lithium immediately.** If there are other signs of lithium toxicity (eg tremors, diarrhoea, vomiting, nausea or confusion) stop lithium and check blood level. Renal and thyroid function should be checked every two to three months when adjusting the dose, and every six months to a year in stable patients.[36]
— Never stop lithium abruptly (except in the presence of toxicity — relapse rates are twice as high under these

conditions.[37] Lithium should be continued for at least six months after symptoms resolve (longer-term use is usually necessary to prevent recurrences).

- Antidepressant medication is often needed during phases of depression but can precipitate mania when used alone (see **'Depression — F32#'**). Bupropion may be less likely than other antidepressants to induce mania.[38] Doses should be as low as possible and used for the shortest time necessary. If the patient becomes hypomanic, stop the antidepressant.

Referral

Referral to secondary mental health services is advised:

- as an emergency if very vulnerable, eg if there is a significant risk of suicide or disruptive behaviour
- urgently if significant depression or mania continues despite treatment.

Non-urgent referral is recommended:

- for assessment, care planning and allocation of key worker under the Care Programme Approach (ref section in intro)
- before starting lithium
- to discuss relapse prevention
- for women on lithium planning pregnancy.

Resources for patients and families

Resource leaflets: 5–1 *Living with bipolar disorder* and 5–2 *Lithium toxicity*.

Manic Depression Fellowship   020 8974 6550
(Advice, support, local self-help groups and publications list for people with manic depressive illness)

Manic Depression Fellowship (Scotland)   0141 331 0344
Booklet: *Inside out: a guide to self-management of manic depression*. Available from the Manic Depression Fellowship, 8–10 High St, Kingston on Thames, KT1 1EY, UK

Workbook: *Living without depression and manic depression: a workbook for maintaining mood stability* by Mary Ellen Copeland. New Harbinger Press, USA. Price: £11.95.

Chronic fatigue and Chronic fatigue syndrome[a] — F48 (may be referred to as 'ME')

Presenting complaints

Patients may report:

- lack of energy
- aches and pains
- feeling tired easily
- an inability to complete tasks.

Diagnostic features

- Mental and physical fatigue, made worse by physical and mental activity.
- Tiredness after minimal effort, with rest bringing little relief.
- Lack of energy.

Other common, often fluctuating, symptoms include:

- dizziness
- headache
- disturbed sleep
- inability to relax
- irritability
- aches and pains eg muscle pain, chest pain, sore throat
- decreased libido
- poor memory and concentration
- depression.

The disorder may be triggered by infection, trauma or other physical illness.

Chronic Fatigue Syndrome is diagnosed when substantial physical and mental fatigue lasts longer than six months, significantly impairs daily activities and where there are no significant findings on physical examination or laboratory investigation. It is associated with other somatic symptoms.[39]

[a] Known internationally as 'Neurasthenia'

Differential diagnosis

- Many medical disorders can cause fatigue. A full history and physical examination is necessary, which can be reassuring for the doctor and therapeutic for the patient. Basic investigations include a full blood count, ESR or CRP, thyroid function tests, urea and electrolytes, liver function tests, blood sugar and C-reactive protein. A medical disorder should be suspected where there is:
  — any abnormal physical finding, eg weight loss
  — any abnormal laboratory finding
  — unusual features of the history, eg recent foreign travel, or the patient is very young or very old
  — symptoms occurring only after exertion and unaccompanied by any features of mental fatigue
- **Depression — F32#** (if low or sad mood is prominent).
- **Chronic mixed anxiety and depression — F41.2**.
- **Panic disorder — F41.1** (if anxiety attacks are prominent).
- **Unexplained somatic complaints — F45** (if unexplained physical symptoms are prominent).

Depression and anxiety may be somatized. Social, relationship or other life problems may cause or exacerbate distress.

Essential information for patient and family

- Periods of fatigue or exhaustion are common and are usually temporary and self-limiting.
- Treatment for chronic fatigue is possible and usually has good results, although the outcome for chronic fatigue syndrome is more variable.[40]

Advice and support to patient and family (R: 6–1, 6–2, 6–3)

- Explore what patients think their symptoms mean. Offer appropriate explanations and reassurance (eg symptoms are genuinely disabling and not 'all in the mind', but that symptoms following exertion do not mean physical damage and long-term disability).
- For chronic fatigue and chronic fatigue syndrome, advise a gradual return to usual activities. This may take time.
- The patient can build endurance with a programme of gradually increasing physical activity. Start with a manageable level and increase a little each week.
- Emphasize pleasant or enjoyable activities. Encourage the patient to resume activities which have helped in the past.

- Discuss sleep patterns. Encourage a regular sleep routine and avoid day time sleep. (See **'Sleep problems [insomnia] — F51'**).
- Avoid excessive rest and/or sudden changes in activity.
- For the much rarer condition of chronic fatigue syndrome, a behavioural approach, including cognitive behavioural therapy, a graded programme of exercise, assessment of and assistance with activities of daily living can be helpful.[41,42] Ideally, this would take place in a primary-care setting using clinical psychologists, nurse practitioners, practice counsellors, physiotherapists, occupational therapists or other suitably trained practitioners.

Medication

- To date, no pharmacological treatment for chronic fatigue has been established.[43]
- Mental disorders (eg depression) are common in chronic fatigue syndrome and may respond to pharmacological treatment. In treating depression, SSRIs (see BNF section 4.3.3) may be neutral or activating, and tricyclics (see BNF section 4.3.1) at full dosage may be sedating.
- In the absence of depression, consider low dose tricyclic antidepressants (eg amitriptyline [50–100 mg a day] or imipramine [20 mg a day]) (see BNF section 4.3.1), which may be effective for pain and poor sleep.[44,45]

Referral

See general referral criteria.

- Consider referral to a physician if the GP is uncertain about diagnosis. (See 'Differential diagnosis' above.)
- Referral to secondary mental-health services, or a liaison psychiatrist, if available, should be considered if there are:
  — other mental disorders, eg eating disorder or bipolar disorder
  — a risk of suicide
  — no improvement despite the above measures.

Resources for patients and their families

Resource leaflets: 6–1 *Chronic tiredness* (for mild to moderate symptoms), 6–2 *Chronic fatigue syndrome* and 6–3 *Dealing with negative thinking in chronic fatigue syndrome* (for more severe symptoms).

Coping with Chronic Fatigue by Trudi Chalder, 1995
(A book with self-help advice)

Chronic Fatigue Syndrome: The Facts by M Sharp and
F Campling, 2000.
(Self-help advice for more severe symptoms)

The Institute of Psychiatry's website (URL:
http://www.smd.kcl.ac.uk/kcsmd/cfs/cfstitle.htm) includes a
full patient-management package for more severe symptoms
of Chronic Fatigue Syndrome. This includes information about
the disorder and suggestions to aid self-management. It is a
useful resource for the practitioner who is working with the
patient to overcome the condition.

Chronic mixed anxiety and depression — F41.2

Presenting complaints
Patient may present with one or more physical symptoms (eg various pains, poor sleep and fatigue), accompanied by a variety of anxiety and depressive symptoms, which will have been present for more than six months. These patients may be well known to their doctors, and have often been treated by a variety of psychotropic agents over the years.

Diagnostic features
- Low or sad mood.
- Loss of interest or pleasure.
- Prominent anxiety or worry.
- Multiple associated symptoms are usually present, eg:
  — disturbed sleep
  — tremor
  — fatigue or loss of energy
  — palpitations
  — poor concentration
  — dizziness
  — disrupted appetite
  — suicidal thoughts or acts
  — dry mouth
  — loss of libido
  — tension and restlessness
  — irritability.

Differential diagnosis
- If more severe symptoms of depression or anxiety are present, see 'Depression — F32#' or 'Generalized anxiety — F41.1'.
- If somatic symptoms predominate that do not appear to have an adequate physical explanation, see 'Unexplained somatic complaints — F45'.
- If the patient has a history of manic episodes (eg excitement, elevated mood and rapid speech), see 'Bipolar disorder — F31'.
- If the patient is drinking heavily or using drugs, see 'Alcohol misuse — F10' and 'Drug use disorders — F11#'. Unexplained

somatic complaints, alcohol or drug disorders may also co-exist with mixed anxiety and depression.

Essential information for patient and family

- Stress or worry have many physical and mental effects, and may be responsible for many of their symptoms. Symptoms are likely to be at their worst at times of personal stress. Aim to help the patient to reduce his or her symptoms.
- These problems are not due to weakness or laziness: patients are trying to cope.
- Regular structured visits can be helpful. State their frequency and include arranged visits to other professionals (to assess progress of any physical disorder and to give any advice on handling life stresses).

Advice and support to patient and family

- If physical symptoms are present, discuss link between physical symptoms and mental distress (see **'Unexplained somatic complaints — F45'**).
- If tension-related symptoms are prominent, advise relaxation methods to relieve physical symptoms. (R: 1–2) ▪
- Advise reduction in caffeine intake[46] and a balanced diet, including plenty of complex carbohydrates and vitamins.[47]
- Discuss ways to challenge negative thoughts or exaggerated worries. (R: 4–2 and 7–3) ▪
- Structured problem-solving methods[48] can help patients to manage current life problems or stresses which contribute to anxiety symptoms (R: 1–1) ▪. Support the patient to carry out the following steps:
  — identifying events that trigger excessive worry. For example, a young woman presents with worry, tension, nausea and insomnia. These symptoms began after her son was diagnosed with asthma. Her anxiety worsens when he has asthma episodes.
  — listing as many possible solutions as the patient can think of (eg meeting with the nurse to learn about asthma management, discussing her concerns with other parents of asthmatic children, writing down a management plan for asthma episodes).
  — listing the advantages and disadvantages of each possible solution. (The patient should do this, perhaps between appointments.)
  — choosing his or her preferred approach.
  — working out the steps necessary to achieve the plan.

— setting a date to review the plan. Identify and reinforce things that are working.

- Help the patient plan activities that are relaxing, distracting or confidence-building. Exercise may be helpful.[49,50] Resume activities that have been helpful in the past.
- Assess risk of suicide. (Has the patient thought frequently about death or dying? Does the patient have a specific suicide plan? Has he/she made serious suicide attempts in the past? Can the patient be sure not to act on suicidal ideas?)
- Encourage self-help books, tapes and/or leaflets.[51] (R: 7–1 and 4–1)

Medication

- Medication should be simplified: medication should be reviewed periodically and the patient should only be prescribed a drug if it is definitely helping. Multiple psychotropics should be avoided.
- An antidepressant with sedative properties can be prescribed if marked symptoms of depression or anxiety are present, but warn of drowsiness and problems driving.[N52] (See BNF section 4.3.) See 'Depression — F32#' for the severity threshold for initiating administration of antidepressants and for specific guidance on the drugs.
- *Hypericum perforata* (known as St John's Wort and available from Health Food Stores) is often taken for milder symptoms of depression.[53] It has mild monoamine oxidase inhibitory properties,[54] so it should not be combined with other antidepressants and caution may be needed with diet.[N55] *Hypericum* is an active agent and interactions with prescribed drugs may occur. See advice from the Committee for Safety of Medicines for further information .[N56]

Referral

See general referral criteria.

Referral to secondary mental-health services is advised:

- as an emergency if suicide risk is significant
- non-urgently for psychological treatments as available.

Consider recommending voluntary/non-statutory/self-help organizations.

Stress/anxiety management,[N57] problem-solving,[N58] cognitive therapy,[59] cognitive behavioural therapy[N60] or counselling,[13] may be helpful and may be provided in primary care or the voluntary sector, as well as secondary mental health services.

C

Resources for patients and families (see also 'Depression — F32#' for more resources)

Resource leaflets: 1–1 *Problem solving*, 1–2 *Learning to relax*, 4–1 *Anxiety and how to reduce it*, 7–1 *Depression and how to cope with it*, 4–2 *Dealing with anxious thoughts* and 7–3 *Dealing with depressive thinking*.

CITA (Council for Involuntary Tranquilliser Addiction) 0151 949 0102

Samaritans   0345 909090 (UK-wide helpline)
(Support by listening for those feeling lonely, despairing or suicidal)
Helping you cope: a guide to starting and stopping tranquillisers and sleeping tablets by the Mental Health Foundation. 020 7580 0145.

Chronic psychotic disorders — F20#

Includes schizophrenia, schizotypal disorder, persistent delusional disorders, induced delusional disorder, other nonorganic psychotic disorders

Presenting complaints

Patients may present with:

- difficulties with thinking or concentration
- reports of hearing voices
- strange beliefs (eg having supernatural powers or being persecuted)
- extraordinary physical complaints (eg having animals or unusual objects inside one's body)
- problems or questions related to antipsychotic medication
- problems in managing work , studies or relationships.

   Families may seek help because of apathy, withdrawal, poor hygiene, or strange behaviour.

Diagnostic features

- Chronic problems with the following features:
  — social withdrawal
  — low motivation, interest or self-neglect
  — disordered thinking (exhibited by strange or disjointed speech).
- Periodic episodes of:
  — agitation or restlessness
  — bizarre behaviour
  — hallucinations (false or imagined perceptions, eg hearing voices)
  — delusions (firm beliefs that are often false, eg patient is related to royalty, receiving messages from television, being followed or persecuted).

Differential diagnosis

- **Depression — F32#** (if low or sad mood, pessimism and/or feelings of guilt).
- **Bipolar disorder — F31** (if symptoms of mania excitement, elevated mood, exaggerated self-worth are prominent).
- **Alcohol misuse — F10** or **Drug use disorders — F11#**. Chronic intoxication or withdrawal from alcohol or other substances (stimulants, hallucinogens) can cause psychotic symptoms.

Patients with chronic psychosis may also abuse drugs and/or alcohol.

Essential information for patient and carer

- Agitation and strange behaviour can be symptoms of a mental illness.
- Symptoms may come and go over time.
- Medication is a central component of treatment; it will both reduce current difficulties and prevent relapse.
- Stable living conditions, (for example, accommodation and income) are a pre-requisite for effective rehabilitation.
- Support of the carer is essential for compliance with treatment and effective rehabilitation. An assessment of the patient's needs and those of the carer (under the Carer's Recognition and Services Act) can be requested from the local Social Services department.
- Voluntary organizations can provide valuable support to the patient and carer.

Advice and support to patient and carer

- Discuss a treatment plan with family members and obtain their support for it, within the confines of medical confidentiality. (R: 10–3)
- Explain that drugs will prevent relapse, and inform patient of side-effects. (R: 1–3)
- Encourage patient to function at the highest reasonable level in work and other daily activities.
- Minimize stress and stimulation:
  - Do not argue with psychotic thinking.
  - Avoid confrontation or criticism.[3]
  - During periods when symptoms are more severe, rest and withdrawal from stress may be helpful.
- Keep the patient's physical health, including health promotion and smoking, under review.[61] Heavy smokers may use tobacco to counteract the sedative effects of their anti-psychotic medication. If this happens, consider a less sedating anti-psychotic.
- If the illness has a relapsing course, work with the patient and family to try to identify early warning signs of relapse. (R: 10–4)
- Encourage the patient to build relationships with key members of the practice team, eg by seeing the same doctor or nurse at each appointment. Use the relationship to discuss the advantages of medication and to review the effectiveness of the care plan. (R: 13–4)

- Refer to '**Acute psychotic disorder — F23**' for advice on the management of agitated or excited states.
- If care is shared with the Community Mental Health Team, agree with them who is to do what.

Medication

- Antipsychotic medication may reduce psychotic symptoms (see BNF section 4.2.1). Examples include haloperidol (1.5–4 mg up to three times a day), or an atypical antipsychotic[N6] (eg olanzapine [5–10 mg a day] or risperidone [4–6 mg per day]). The dose should be the lowest possible for relief of symptoms. The drugs have different side-effect profiles. Indications for atypical drugs include uncontrolled acute extrapyramidal effects, uncontrolled hyperprolactinaemia and predominant, unresponsive, negative symptoms (eg withdrawal and low motivation). More information on side-effect profiles can be found in the *Maudsley Prescribing Guidelines*.[10] Inform the patient that continued medication will reduce risk of relapse. In general, antipsychotic medication should be continued for at least six months, following a first episode of illness, and longer after a subsequent episode.[N9]
- If, after team support, the patient is reluctant or erratic in taking medication, injectable long-acting antipsychotic medication may be considered in order to ensure continuity of treatment and reduce risk of relapse.[62] It should be reviewed at four- to six-monthly intervals. Doctors and nurses who give depot injections in primary care need training to do so.[63] If available, specific counselling about medication also is helpful.[64] As part of the 'shared care plan', decide who is to contact the patient should he or she fail to attend an appointment.
- Discuss potential side-effects with the patient. Common motor side-effects include:
  — Acute dystonias or spasms that can be managed with antiparkinsonian drugs (eg procyclidine [5 mg three times per day] or orphenadrine [50 mg three times per day]). (See BNF section 4.9.)
  — Parkinsonian symptoms (eg tremor and akinesia), which can be managed with oral antiparkinsonian drugs (see BNF section 4.9) (eg procylidine [5 mg up to three times a day] or orphenadrine [50 mg three times per day]). Withdrawal of antiparkinsonian drugs should be attempted after two to three months without symptoms, as these drugs are liable to misuse and may impair memory.
  Akathisia (severe motor restlessness) may be managed with

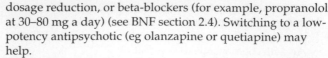

dosage reduction, or beta-blockers (for example, propranolol at 30–80 mg a day) (see BNF section 2.4). Switching to a low-potency antipsychotic (eg olanzapine or quetiapine) may help.

- Other possible side-effects include weight gain, galactorrhoea and photosensitivity. Patients suffering from drug-induced photosensitivity are eligible for sunscreen on prescription.

Referral

Referral to secondary mental-health services is advised:

- urgently, if there are signs of relapse, unless there is an established previous response to treatment and it is safe to manage the patient at home.
- non-urgently:
  — to clarify diagnosis and ensure most appropriate treatment
  — if there is non-compliance with treatment, problematic side-effects, failure of community treatment or breakdown of living arrangements (eg threat of loss of home)
  — for all new practice patients with diagnosis of psychosis for review.

Patients with a range of mental-health, occupational, social and financial needs are normally managed by specialist services. Referral for a key worker under the Care Programme approach should always be considered.

Community Mental Health Services may be able to provide compliance therapy,[N64] family interventions,[N65] cognitive behaviour therapy[66] and rehabilitative facilities.

Resources for patients and families

Resource leaflets: 1–3 *Coping with the side-effects of medication*, 10–2 *About schizophrenia*, 10–3 *Coping with difficult behaviours* and 10–4 *Early warning signs* form.

National Schizophrenia Fellowship　020 8974 6814
(Advice line: 10.30 am–3 pm)

National Schizophrenia Fellowship (Scotland)
0131 557 8969

National Schizophrenia Fellowship (Northern Ireland)
02890 402 323

MINDinfoLINE　0345 660 163 (outside London) 020 85221728
(Greater London)

SANELine　0345 678 000 (seven nights, 2 pm–midnight)

Hearing Voices Network　0161 228 3896
(Monday–Wednesday, Friday 10.30 am– 3 pm)
(Self-help groups to allow people to explore their voice hearing experiences)

Healthy Living with Schizophrenia by the Health Education Authority, 020 7413 1991

Working with Voices by R Coleman and M Smith. Handsell, 1997
(Workbook to help voice hearers manage their voices.)

Living With Schizophrenia: a Holistic Approach to Understanding, Preventing and Recovering from Negative Symptoms by John Watkins. Hill of Content, 1996.

Delirium — F05

Presenting complaints
- Families may request help because patient is confused or agitated.
- Patients may appear uncooperative or fearful.
- Delirium may occur in patients hospitalised for physical conditions.

Diagnostic features
Acute onset, usually over hours or days, of:
- confusion (patient appears disoriented and struggles to understand surroundings)
- clouded thinking or awareness.

This is often accompanied by:

- poor memory
- agitation
- emotional upset
- loss of orientation
- wandering attention
- hearing voices

- withdrawal from others
- visions or illusions
- suspiciousness
- disturbed sleep (reversal of sleep pattern).
- autonomic features (eg sweating, tachycardia)

Symptoms often develop rapidly and may change from hour to hour.

Delerium may occur in patients with previously normal mental function or in those with dementia. Milder stresses (eg medication and mild infections) may cause delirium in older patients or in those with dementia.

Differential diagnosis
Identify and correct possible, underlying physical causes of delirium, such as:

- alcohol intoxication or withdrawal
- drug intoxication, overdose or withdrawal (including prescribed drugs)
- infection
- metabolic changes (eg liver disease, dehydration, hypoglycaemia)
- head trauma
- hypoxia

- epilepsy.

If symptoms persist, delusions and disordered thinking predominate, and no physical cause is identified, see '**Acute psychotic disorders — F23**'.

Essential information for patient and family
- Strange behaviour or speech and confusion can be symptoms of a medical illness.

Advice and support to patient and family[67]
- Take measures to prevent the patient from harming him/herself or others (eg remove unsafe objects, restrain if necessary).
- Supportive contact with familiar people can reduce confusion.
- Provide frequent reminders of time and place to reduce confusion.
- Hospitalization may be required because of agitation or because of the physical illness which is causing delirum. There is an appreciable mortality with delirium. Patient may need to be admitted to a medical ward in order to diagnose and treat the underlying disorder. In an emergency, where there is risk to life and safety, a medically ill patient may be taken to a general hospital for treatment under common law, without using the Mental Health Act. In such a case, a medical doctor may make this decision without involvement of a psychiatrist.

Medication[68]
- Avoid use of sedative or hypnotic medications (eg benzodiazepines) except for the treatment of alcohol or sedative withdrawal).
- Antipsychotic medication in low doses (see BNF section 4.2.1) may sometimes be needed to control agitation, psychotic symptoms or aggression. Beware of drug side-effects (drugs with anticholinergic action and antiparkinsonian medication can exacerbate or cause delirium) and drug interactions.

Referral
Referral to secondary mental-health services is rarely indicated. Referral to a physician is nearly always indicated if:

- the cause is unclear
- the cause is clear and treatable, but carers are unable to support the patient, or he/she is living alone
- drug or alcohol withdrawal or overdose or another underlying condition necessitating inpatient medical care is suspected.

Dementia — FOO#

Presenting complaints

- Patients may complain of forgetfulness, decline in mental functioning, or feeling depressed, but may be unaware of memory loss. Patients and family may sometimes deny, or be unaware of, severity of memory loss and other deterioration in function.
- Families may ask for help initially because of failing memory, disorientation, change in personality or behaviour. In the later stages of the illness, they may seek help because of behavioural disturbance, wandering or incontinence or an episode of dangerous behaviour (eg leaving the gas on unlit).
- Dementia may also be diagnosed during consultations for other problems, as relatives may believe deterioration in memory and function are a natural part of ageing.
- Changes in behaviour and functioning (eg poor personal hygiene or social interaction) in an older patient should raise the possibility of a diagnosis of dementia.

Diagnostic features

- Decline in memory for recent events, thinking, judgement, orientation and language.
- Patients may have become apparently apathetic or disinterested, but may also appear alert and appropriate despite deterioration in memory and other cognitive function.
- Decline in everyday functioning (eg dressing, washing, cooking).
- Changes in personality or emotional control — patients may become easily upset, tearful or irritable, as well as apathetic.
- Common with advancing age (5% over 65 years; 20% over 80 years),[69] very rare in youth or middle age.

Progression is classically 'stepwise' in vascular dementia, gradual in Alzheimers's and fluctuating in Lewy-Body dementia (fluctuating cognition, visual hallucinations and parkinsonism) but the clinical picture is often not clear cut.

Owing to the problems inherent in taking a history from people with dementia, it is very important that information about the level of current functioning and possible decline in functioning should also be obtained from an informant (eg spouse, child or other carer).

Tests of memory and thinking include:

- ability to repeat the names of three common objects (eg apple, table, penny) immediately and recall them after three minutes
- ability to accurately identify the day of the week, the month and the year
- ability to give their name and full, postal address

A very short screening test is set out in the resource section on the disc. (R: 13–3) 🖫

Differential diagnosis

Examine and investigate for treatable causes of dementia. Common causes of cognitive worsening in the elderly are:

- urinary tract, chest, skin or ear infection
- onset or exacerbation of cardiac failure
- prescribed drugs, especially psychiatric and antiparkinsonian drugs, and alcohol
- cerebrovascular ischaemia or hypoxia.

Less common causes include:

- severe depression mimicking dementia
- severe anaemia in the very old
- vitamin B_{12} or folate deficiency
- hypothyroidism
- slow-growing cerebral tumour
- renal failure
- communicating hydrocephalus.

Sudden increases in confusion, wandering attention or agitation will usually indicate a physical illness (eg acute infectious illness) or toxicity from medication. See 'Delirium — F05'.

Depression may cause memory and concentration problems similar to those of dementia, especially in older patients. If low or sad mood is prominent, or if the impairment is patchy and has developed rapidly, see 'Depression — F32#'.

Helpful tests: MSU, FBC, B_{12}, Folate, LFTs, TFTs, U and E, and glucose.

Essential information for patient and family

- Dementia is frequent in old age but is not inevitable.
- Memory loss and confusion may cause behaviour problems (eg agitation, suspiciousness, emotional outbursts, apathy and inability to take part in normal social interaction).

- Memory loss usually proceeds slowly, but the course and long-term prognosis varies with the disease causing dementia. Discuss diagnosis, likely progress and prognosis with the patient and family.
- Physical illness or other stresses can increase confusion.
- The patient will have great difficulty in learning new information. Avoid placing patient in unfamiliar places or situations.
- Membership of a support group and information on dementia for the family can aid caring.

Always give information about local services in addition to general advice about dementia.

Advice and support to patient and family

- Regularly review the patient's ability to perform daily tasks safely, behavioural problems and general physical condition.
- If memory loss is mild, consider use of memory aids or reminders.
- Encourage the patient to make full use of remaining abilities.
- Encourage maintainance of the patient's physical health and fitness through good diet and exercise, plus swift treatment of intercurrent physical illness..
- Make sure the patient and family understand that the condition may impair ability to drive. If the patient is incapable of understanding this advice, the GP should inform the DVLA immediately.
- Regularly assess risk (balancing safety and independence), especially at times of crisis. As appropriate, discuss arrangements for support in the home, community or day care programmes, or residential placement.
- Review how the carer is managing, especially if they live together. Consider ways to reduce stress on those caring for the patient (eg self-help groups, home help, day care and respite care). Contact with other families caring for relatives with dementia may be helpful. An assessment of the patient's needs and those of the carer (under the Carer's Recognition and Services Act) can be requested from the local Social Services Department. Carers may need continuing support after the patient has entered residential care or has died.
- Discuss planning of legal and financial affairs. Attendance allowance and a discount on council tax bills can usually be claimed. An information sheet is available from the Alzheimer's Society (see 'Resources for patients and families') and further

information and help can be obtained through local Social Services.

Medication

- Try non-pharmacological methods of dealing with difficult behaviour first. For example, carers may be able to deal with repetitive questioning if they are given the information that this is because of the dementia affecting the patient's memory.
- Antipsychotic medication in very low doses (see BNF section 4.2.1) may sometimes be needed to manage some behavioural problems (eg aggression or restlessness). Behavioural problems change with the course of the dementia; therefore, withdraw medication every few months on a trial basis to see if it is still needed, and discontinue if it is not. Beware of drug side-effects (eg parkinsonian symptoms, anticholinergic effects) and drug interactions (avoid combining with tricyclic antidepressants, alcohol, anticonvulsants or L-dopa preparations.). Antipsychotics should be avoided in Lewy-Body dementia.[70]
- Avoid using sedative or hypnotic medications (eg benzodiazepines) if possible. If other treatments have failed and severe management problems remain, use very cautiously and for no more than two weeks; they may increase confusion.
- Aspirin in low doses may be prescribed in vascular dementia to attempt to slow deterioration.
- In Alzheimer's disease, consider referring to secondary care for assessment and initiation of anticholinesterase drugs[71] depending on locally agreed policies.

Referral

- Refer to a specialist to confirm diagnosis in complicated or atypical cases.
- Consider referral to social services for practical help: needs assessment, formal care planning, home help and day care and help with placement and benefits.
- Refer to a physician if complex medical co-morbidity or sudden worsening of dementia.
- Refer to psychiatric services if there are intractable behavioural problems, unusually complex family relationships or if depressive or psychotic episode occurs.

Resources for patients and familes

Alzheimer's Society and CJD Support Network
020 7306 0606
(Support to family and friends of people with dementia of all
kinds – ie not just Alzheimer's)

Age Concern England   0800 00 99 66
(Information and advice relating to older people) 020 8679 8000

Age Concern Northern Ireland   02890 245729

Age Concern Cymru   029 2037 1566

Age Concern Scotland   0131 220 3345

Help the Aged   020 7253 0253

Association of Crossroads Care Attendants Scheme
01788 573653
(Regional centres throughout UK providing practical support
and help for carers)

Counsel and Care   020 7485 1566 (10.30 am–4 pm)
(Advice and information on home and residential care for
older people)

Benefits Enquiry Line   0800 882200

Carer's Line   0808 808 7777

Carer's National Association   020 7490 8818

Alzheimer's at your Fingertips by Harry Cayton, Dr Nori
Graham and Dr J Warner. Class Publishing, 1997, £11.95.
(This is a good book for patients and carers, answering
commonly asked questions about all types of dementia.)

Depression — F32#

Presenting complaints

The patient may present initially with one or more physical symptoms, such as pain or 'tiredness all the time'. Further enquiry will reveal low mood or loss of interest.

Irritability is sometimes the presenting problem.

A wide range of presenting complaints may accompany or conceal depression. These include anxiety or insomnia, worries about social problems such as financial or marital difficulties, increased drug or alcohol use, or (in a new mother) constant worries about her baby or fear of harming the baby.

Some groups are at higher risk (eg those who have recently given birth or had a stroke, and those with physical disorders, eg Parkinson's disease or multiple sclerosis).

Diagnostic features
- Low or sad mood
- Loss of interest or pleasure.

At least four of the following associated symptoms are present:

- disturbed sleep
- disturbed appetite
- guilt or low self-worth
- pessimism or hopelessness about the future
- decreased libido
- diurnal mood variation

- poor concentration
- suicidal thoughts or acts
- loss of self confidence
- fatigue or loss of energy
- agitation or slowing of movement or speech

Symptoms of anxiety or nervousness are also frequently present.

Differential diagnosis
- **Acute psychotic disorder — F23** (if hallucinations [eg hearing voices] or delusions [eg strange or unusual beliefs] are present).
- **Bipolar disorder — F31** (if patient has a history of manic episodes [eg excitement, rapid speech, elevated mood]).
- **Alcohol misuse — F10** or **Drug use disorder — F11#** (if heavy alcohol or drug use is present).
- **Chronic mixed anxiety and depression — F41.2**.

55

Some medications may produce symptoms of depression (eg beta-blockers, other antihypertensives, H2 blockers, oral contraceptives, corticosteroids).

Unexplained somatic complaints, anxiety, alcohol or drug disorders may co-exist with depression.

Essential information for patient and family

- Depression is a common illness and effective treatments are available.
- Depression is not weakness or laziness.
- Depression can affect patients' ability to cope.
- Recommend information leaflets or audiotapes to reinforce the information. (R: 7–1)

Advice and support to patient and family

- Assess risk of suicide. Ask a series of questions about suicidal ideas, plans and intent (eg has the patient often thought of death or dying? Does the patient have a specific suicide plan? Has he/she made serious suicide attempts in the past? Can the patient be sure not to act on suicidal ideas?) Close supervision by family or friends, or hospitalization may be needed. Ask about risk of harm to others. Consider high-risk groups, eg older people, men, those with physical illness, substance abuse, a family history of suicide, or those who have demonstrated self-harm previously.
- Identify current life problems or social stresses, including precipitating factors. Focus on small, specific steps patients might take towards reducing or improving managment of these problems. Avoid major decisions or life changes. (R: 1–1)
- Plan short-term activities which give the patient enjoyment or build confidence. Exercise may be helpful.[72]
- If appropriate, advise reduction in caffeine intake[46] and drug and alcohol use.[73]
- Support the development of good sleep patterns and encourage a balanced diet.[47]
- Encourage the patient to resist pessimism and self-criticism and not to act on pessimistic ideas (eg ending marriage, leaving job), and not to concentrate on negative or guilty thoughts.
- If physical symptoms are present, discuss the link between physical symptoms and mood (see **'Unexplained somatic symptoms — F45'**).
- Involve the patient in discussing the advantages and disadvantages of available treatments. Inform the patient that medication usually works more quickly than

psychotherapies.[N74,75] Where a patient chooses not to take medication, respect their decision and arrange another appointment to monitor progress.
- After improvement, plan with patient the action to be taken if signs of relapse occur.

Medication

Consider antidepressant drugs if sad mood or loss of interest are prominent for at least two weeks, and if four or more of these symptoms are present:

- fatigue or loss of energy
- disturbed sleep
- guilt or self-reproach
- poor concentration
- thoughts of death or suicide
- disturbed appetite
- agitation or slowing of movement and speech.

There is no evidence that people with only few or very mild depressive symptoms respond to antidepressants.[76]

Consider medication at the first visit.

At present, there is no evidence to suggest that any antidepressant is more effective than others.[77,78] However, their side-effect profiles differ and therefore some drugs will be more acceptable to particular patients than others. (See BNF section 4.3.)

Choice of medication:

- If the patient has responded well to a particular drug in the past, use that drug again.
- If the patient is older or physically ill, use medication with fewer anticholinergic and cardiovascular side-effects.
- If the patient is suicidal, avoid tricyclics and consider dispensing a few days supply at a time.
- If the patient is anxious or unable to sleep, use a drug with more sedative effects, but warn of drowsiness and problems driving.
- If the patient is unwilling to give up alcohol, choose one of the SSRI antidepressants which do not interact with alcohol (currently fluoxetine, paroxetine and citalopram). (See BNF section 4.3.3.)
- *Hypericum perforata* (St. John's Wort) is often taken for milder symptoms of depression, both acute and chronic.[53] It has mild MAOI properties,[54] so it should not be combined with other antidepressants and caution may be needed with diet.[N55] *Hypericum* is an active agent and interactions with prescribed drugs may occur. See advice from the Committee for Safety of Medicines for further information .[N56]

Explain to the patient that:

- the medication must be taken every day
- the drug is not addictive
- improvement will build up over two to three weeks after starting the medication
- mild side-effects may occur but usually fade in seven to 10 days.

Stress that the patient should consult the doctor before stopping the medication. All antidepressants should be withdrawn slowly, preferably over four weeks in weekly decrements.

Continue full-dose antidepressant medication for at least four to six months after the condition improves to prevent relapse.[79,80] Review regularly during this time. Consider, with the patient, the need for futher continuation beyond four to six months.

If patient has had several episodes of major depression, consider carefully long-term, prophylactic treatment.[N81] Obtain a second opinion at this point, if available.

If sleep problems are very severe, consider the use of hypnotics in the short term — no longer than two weeks — in addition to an antidepressant. A sedative tricyclic is often sufficient but, if not, a short-term hynotic may be helpful.

If using tricyclic medication, build up to the effective dose over seven to 10 days. For example, dothiepin: start at 50–75 mg and build to 150 mg nocte; imipramine: start at 25–50 mg each night and build to 100–150 mg).[82]

Withdraw antidepressant medication slowly, and monitor for withdrawal reactions and to ensure remission is stable. Gradual reduction of SSRIs can be achieved by using syrup in reducing doses or taking a tablet on alternate days.

Referral

The following structured therapies, delivered by properly trained practitioners, have been shown to be effective for some people with depression:

- Cognitive behavioural therapy (CBT)[N83]
- behaviour therapy[N83]
- interpersonal therapy[N83]
- structured problem-solving.[N83]

Patients with chronic, relapsing depression may benefit more from CBT or a combination of CBT and antidepressants than from medication alone.[84,85] Counselling may be helpful, especially in milder cases and if focused on specific psychosocial problems which are related to the depression (eg relationships, bereavement).[N13]

Referral to secondary mental-health services is advised:

- as an emergency, if there is a significant risk of suicide or danger to others, psychotic symptoms or severe agitation .
- as a non-emergency, if significant depression persists despite treatment in primary care. (Antidepressant therapy has failed if the patient remains symptomatic after a full course of treatment at an adequate dosage. If there is no clear improvement with the first drug, it should be changed to another class of drug.)

If drug or alcohol misuse is also a problem, see the guidelines for these disorders.

Recommend voluntary/non-statutory services in all other cases where symptoms persist, where the patient has a poor or non-existent support network, or where social or relationship problems are contributing to the depression.[86]

Severely depressed adolescents are difficult to assess and manage, and referral is recommended.

Resources for patients and families

Resource leaflets: 1–1 *Problem solving*, 7–1 *Depression and how to cope with it*, 7.3 *Dealing with depressive thinking* and 7–4 *MAOI diet sheet*.

UK Register of Counsellors   01788 568739
(Provides list of BAC accredited counsellors)

Depression Alliance   020 7633 9929 Answerphone

Samaritans   0345 909090

Association for Post Natal Illness   020 7386 0868

SAD (Seasonal Affective Disorder) Association   01903 814942

Depression: way out of your prison by Dorothy Rowe.
(Explanatory book)
So young, so sad, so listen by Graham P and Hughes C. Gaskell Press, 1995. £5. (A book covering childhood depression)
Coping with postnatal depression by Fiona Marshall. Sheldon Press.

Dissociative (conversion) disorder — F44

Presenting complaints

Patients exhibit unusual or dramatic physical symptoms, such as seizures, amnesia, trance, loss of sensation, visual disturbances, paralysis, aphonia, identity confusion or 'possession' states. The patient is not aware of their role in their symptoms — they are not malingering.

Diagnostic features

Physical symptoms that are:

- unusual in presentation
- not consistent with known disease.

Onset is often sudden and related to psychological stress or difficult personal circumstances.

In acute cases, symptoms may:

- be dramatic and unusual
- change from time to time
- be related to attention from others.

In more chronic cases, patients may appear unduly calm in view of the seriousness of the complaint.

Differential diagnosis

Carefully consider physical conditions that may cause symptoms. A full history and physical (including neurological) examination are essential. Early symptoms of neurological disorders (eg multiple sclerosis) may resemble conversion symptoms.

- If other unexplained physical symptoms are present, see 'Unexplained somatic complaints — F45'.
- Depression — F32#. Atypical depression may present in this way.

Essential information for patient and family

- Physical or neurological symptoms often have no clear physical cause. Symptoms can be brought about by stress.
- Symptoms usually resolve rapidly (from hours to a few weeks), leaving no permanent damage.

Advice and support to patient and family

- Encourage the patient to acknowledge recent stresses or difficulties (though it is not necessary for the patient to link the stresses to current symptoms).
- Give positive reinforcement for improvement. Try not to reinforce symptoms.
- Advise the patient to take a brief rest and relief from stress, then return to usual activities.
- Advise against prolonged rest or withdrawal from activities.

Medication

Avoid anxiolytics or sedatives.

In more chronic cases with depressive symptoms, antidepressant medication may be helpful.

Referral

See general referral criteria.

Non-urgent referral to secondary mental health services is advised if confident of the diagnosis:

- if symptoms persist
- if symptoms are recurrent or severe
- if the patient is prepared to discuss a psychological contribution to symptoms.

If unsure of the diagnosis, consider referral to a physician before referral to secondary mental-health services.

Resources for patients and their families

UK Register of Counsellors 01788 568739
(Supplies names and addresses of BAC-accredited counsellors).

Drug use disorders — F11#

Presenting complaints

Patients may have depressed mood, nervousness or insomnia.

Patients may present with a direct request for prescriptions for narcotics or other drugs, a request for help to withdraw, or for help with stabilising their drug use.

They may present in a state of intoxication or withdrawal or with physical complications of drug use, eg abscesses or thromboses. They may also present with social or legal consequences of their drug use, eg debt or prosecution. Occasionally, covert drug use may manifest itself as bizarre, unexplained behaviour.

Signs of drug withdrawal include:

• Opioids: nausea, sweating, hallucinations
• Sedatives: anxiety, tremors, hallucinations
• Stimulants: depression, moodiness.

Family may request help before the patient (eg because the patient is irritable at home or missing work.)

Whatever their motivation for seeking help, the aim of treatment is to assist the patient to remain healthy until, if motivated to do so and with appropriate help and support, he or she can achieve a drug-free life.

Diagnostic features

• Drug use has caused physical harm (eg injuries while intoxicated), psychological harm (eg symptoms of mental disorder due to drug use), or has led to harmful social consequences (eg loss of job, severe family problems, or criminality).
• Habitual and/or harmful or chaotic drug use.
• Difficulty controlling drug use.
• Strong desire to use drugs.
• Tolerance (can use large amounts of drugs without appearing intoxicated).
• Withdrawal (eg anxiety, tremors or other withdrawal symptoms after stopping use).

Diagnosis will be aided by:

- History — including reason for presentation, past and current (ie in the past four weeks) drug use, history of injecting and risk of HIV and hepatitis, past medical and psychiatric history, social (and especially child care) responsibilities, forensic history and past contact with treatment services
- Examination — motivation, physical (needle tracks, complications, eg thrombosis or viral illness), mental state
- Investigations (haemoglobin, LFTs, urine drug screen, hepatitis B and C).

Differential diagnosis

- **Alcohol misuse — F10** often co-exists. Polydrug use is common.
- Symptoms of anxiety or depression may also occur with heavy drug use. If these continue after a period of abstinence (eg about four weeks), see 'Depression — F32#' and 'Generalized anxiety — F41.1'
- **Psychotic disorders — F23, F20#**.
- Acute organic syndromes.

Essential information for patient and family

- Drug misuse is a chronic, relapsing problem, and controlling, or stopping, use often requires several attempts. Relapse is common.
- Abstinence should be seen as the long-term goal. Harm reduction (especially reducing intravenous drug use) may be a more realistic goal in the short- to medium term.
- Ceasing or reducing drug-use will bring psychological, social and physical benefits.
- Using some drugs during pregnancy risks harming the baby.[N87]
- For intravenous drug-users, there is a risk of transmitting HIV infection, hepatitis or other infections carried by body fluids. Discuss appropriate precautions (eg use condoms, and do not share needles, syringes, spoons, water or any other injecting equipment).
- Doctors are advised to notify new presentations by completion of the regional database form.

Advice and support to patient and family

Advice should be given according to the patient's motivation and willingness to change.[88] For many patients with chronic, relapsing opioid dependence, the treatment of choice is maintenance on long-acting opioids.[89]

For all patients:

- discuss costs and benefits of drug-use from the patient's perspective

- feedback information about health risks, including the results of investigations
- emphasize personal responsibility for change
- give clear advice to change
- assess and manage physical health problems (eg anaemia, chest problems) and nutritional deficiencies
- consider options for problem solving, or targeted counselling, to deal with life problems related to drug use.

For patients not willing to stop or change drug use now:

- Do not reject or blame.
- Advise on harm-reduction strategies (eg if the patient is injecting, advise on needle exchange, not injecting alone, not mixing alcohol, benzodiazepines and opiates). (R: 8–1) 💾
- Clearly point out medical, psychological and social problems caused by drugs.
- Make a future appointment to reassess health (eg well-woman checks, immunization) and discuss drug use.

If reducing drug-use is a reasonable goal (or if a patient is unwilling to quit):

- negotiate a clear goal for decreased use (eg no more than one marijuana cigarette per day with two drug-free days per week)
- discuss strategies to avoid or cope with high-risk situations (eg social situations or stressful events).
- introduce self-monitoring procedures (eg diary of drug use) (R: 8–2) 💾 , and safer drug-use behaviours (eg time restrictions, slowing down rate of use)
- consider options for counselling and/or rehabilitation.

If maintenance on substitute drugs is a reasonable goal (or if a patient is unwilling to quit):

- negotiate a clear goal for less harmful behaviour. Help the patient develop a hierarchy of aims (eg reduction of injecting behaviour, cessation of illicit use and maintenance on prescribed, substitute drugs)
- discuss strategies to avoid or cope with high-risk situations (eg social situations or stressful events)
- consider withdrawal symptoms and how to avoid or reduce them. Provide information on the recognition and management of methadone toxicity
- consider options for counselling and/or rehabilitation.

For patients willing to stop now:

64
- set a definite day to quit

- consider withdrawal symptoms and how to manage them
- discuss strategies to avoid or cope with high-risk situations (eg social situations or stressful events)
- make specific plans to avoid drug use (eg how to respond to friends who still use drugs)
- identify family or friends who will support stopping drug-use
- consider options for counselling and/or rehabilitation.

For patients who do not succeed, or who relapse:

- identify and give credit for any success
- discuss situations which led to relapse
- return to earlier steps.

Self-help organizations (eg Narcotics Anonymous) are often helpful.

Medication

To withdraw a patient from benzodiazepines, convert to a long-acting drug such as diazepam and reduce gradually (eg by 2 mg per fortnight) over a period of two to six months (see BNF section 4.1). See *Guidelines for the prevention and treatment of benzodiazepine dependence*[90] for more information.

Withdrawal from stimulants or cocaine is distressing, and may require medical supervision under a shared-care scheme.

Both long-term maintenance of a patient on substitute opiates (eg methadone) and withdrawal from opiates should be done as part of a shared-care scheme.[91] A multidisciplinary approach is essential and should include drug counselling/therapy[N92] and possible future rehabilitation needs.[93] The doctor signing the prescription is solely responsible for prescribing; this cannot be delegated. See the Department of Health's document, *Drug Misuse Guidelines on Clinical Management*,[94] for more information.

- Careful assessment, including urine analysis and, where possible, dose assessment is essential before prescribing any substitute medication, including methadone. Addicts often try and obtain a higher-than-needed dose. Dosages will depend on the results of this assessment.
- For long-term maintenance or stabilization prior to gradual withdrawal, the dose should be titrated up to that needed to both block withdrawal symptoms and block craving for opiates.[N95]
- For gradual withdrawal, after a period of stabilization, the drug can be slowly tapered, eg by 5 mg a fortnight.
- Daily dispensing (using blue FP 10 prescription forms) and, where available, supervised ingestion, are recommended,

especially in the first three months of treatment. Record exact details of the prescription, frequency and chemist in case the patient presents to a colleague.

- In the UK, at the present time, Methadone Mixture BNF at 1 mg/ml is the most-often used substitute medication for opioid addiction[96] (see BNF section 4.10). Other, newer drugs are, or may become, available (eg Buprenorphine[97]). Specialist advice should be obtained before prescribing these.
- Withdrawal from opiates for patients whose drug-use is already well controlled can be managed with Lofexidine,[98,99] (see BNF section 4.10).

Referral

Help with life problems, employment, social relationships, is an important component of treatment.[100]

Shared care between all agencies (non statutory agencies, NHS mental health and drug misuse services) and professionals involved is essential. Clarity on who is responsible for prescribing and for the physical care of the patient is crucial. The Substance Abuse Advisory Service (SMAS) (Tel: 020 7881 9255) can provide advice and has a primary care shared care network.

Resources for patients and their familes

Resource leaflets: 8–1 *Harm minimization advice* and 8–2 *Drug-use diary*

Narcotics Anonymous   020 7730 0009

CITA (Council for Involuntary Tranquilliser Addiction)
0151 949 0102 (Monday–Friday, 9.30 am–4.45 pm)

ADFAM National   020 7928 8900
(Helpline for families and friends of drug-users)

National Drugs Helpline   0800 776600
(Provides 24-hr, free, confidential advice, including information on local services)

Release   020 7603 8654 (24-hr helpline)
       020 7729 9904 (Advice line, 10 am–6 pm)
       0808 8000 800 (**Drugs in School Helpline**, 10 am–6 pm)
(Advice, support and information to drug-users, their friends and families on all aspects of drug use and drug-related legal problems).

Eating disorders — F50

Presenting complaints

The patient may indulge in binge-eating and extreme weight-control measures such as self-induced vomiting, excessive use of diet pills and laxative abuse.

The family may ask for help because of the patient's loss of weight, refusal to eat, vomiting or amenorrhoea.

Both anorexia and bulimia may present as physical disorders (eg amenorrhoea, seizures, or cardiac arrhythmias that require monitoring or treatment).

Diagnostic features

Common features are:

- unreasonable fear of being fat or gaining weight
- extensive efforts to control weight (eg strict dieting, vomiting, use of purgatives, excessive exercise)
- denial that weight or eating habits are a problem
- low mood, anxiety/irritability
- obsessional symptoms
- relationship difficulties
- increasing withdrawal
- school and work problems.

Patients with anorexia nervosa typically show:

- severe dieting, despite very low weight (BMI [body mass index] <17.5 kg/m^2)
- distorted body image (ie an unreasonable belief that one is overweight)
- amenorrhoea.

Patients with bulimia typically show:

- binge-eating (ie eating large amounts of food in a few hours)
- purging (attempts to eliminate food by self-induced vomiting, or via diuretic or laxative use)

A patient may show both anorexic and bulimic patterns at different times.

Differential diagnosis

- Depression — F32# may occur along with bulimia or anorexia.   67

- Physical illness may cause weight loss.
- There may be co-existing problems such as drugs and alcohol misuse or self harm.

Medical consequences of severe weight loss include amenorrhea, dental problems, muscle weakness, renal stones, constipation and liver dysfunction. Medical complications of purging include dental problems, salivary-gland swelling, kidney stones, cardiac arrhythmias and seizures.

Essential information for patient and family

- Purging and severe starvation may cause serious physical harm. Anorexia nervosa can be life-threatening.
- Purging and severe dieting are ineffective ways of achieving lasting weight-control.
- Self-help groups, leaflets and books may be helpful in explaining the diagnosis clearly and involving the patient in treatment.

Advice and support to patient and family

The GP can undertake simple steps to treat eating disorders with the help of the practice counsellor, practice nurse and/or a dietician.

In anorexia nervosa:

- It is helpful to see the patient without, as well as with, the family.
- Expect denial and ambivalence. Elicit the patient's concerns about the negative effects of anorexia nervosa on aspects of their life. Ask the patient about the benefits that anorexia has for them (eg feeling of being in control, feeling safe, being able to get care and attention from family). Don't try to force the patient to change if he or she is not ready.
- Educate the patient about food and weight.
- Weigh the patient regularly and chart their weight. Set manageable goals in agreement with the patient (eg aim for a 0.5 kg weight increase per week [this requires a calorie intake of about 2500 kcal per day]). A supportive family member may be able to help the patient achieve this. Consultation with a dietician may be helpful to establish normal calorie and nutrient intake and regular patterns of eating.
- A return to normal eating habits may be a distant goal.
- Provide counselling, if available, regarding traumatic life events and difficulties (past and present) which seem significant in the onset or maintainance of the disorder.

- Encourage the family to be patient and consistent.

  In bulimia nervosa:

- Use a collaborative approach.
- A food diary can be a useful therapeutic tool, in discussions with the patient. (R: 9–1)🖐
- Educate the patient about the need to eat regularly throughout the day (three meals, plus two snacks) to reduce urges to binge.
- Set mutually agreed, gradual goals to increase the number of meals eaten, the variety of foods allowed and to reduce vomiting and the use of laxatives.
- Help patient identify psychological and physiological triggers for binge eating and make clear plans to cope more effectively with these trigger events (eg plan alternative behaviour). (R: 9–2)🖐
- Discuss the patient's biased beliefs about weight, shape and eating (eg carbohydrates are fattening) and encourage review of rigid views about body image (eg patients believe no one will like them unless they are very thin). Do not simply state that the patient's view is wrong.
- Provide counselling, if available, regarding difficulties underlying or maintaining the disorder (eg childhood abuse, relationship difficulties, or concurrent problems with substance abuse).

Medication

- In bulimia nervosa, antidepressants (eg fluoxetine at 60 mg) are effective in reducing binging and vomiting in a proportion of cases;[N101] however, compliance with medication may be poor. (See BNF section 4.3.)
- No pharmacological treatment for anorexia has been established to date.[N102] Psychiatric conditions (eg depression) may co-occur and may respond to pharmacological treatment.
- Order blood tests for urea and electrolytes.

Referral

Refer for urgent assessment (if possible, to secondary mental-health services with expertise in eating disorders) if:

- body mass index is <13.5 kg/m^2, especially if there has been rapid weight-loss. (BMI = weight in kilograms/height in metres^2)
- potassium levels are <2.5 mmol/l
- there is severe bone-marrow dysfunction, with loss of platelets
- there is evidence of proximal myopathy

- there are significant gastrointestinal symptoms from repeated vomiting (eg blood in vomitus)
- there is significant risk of suicide
- there are other complicating factors (eg substance or alcohol abuse).

Refer to secondary mental-health services for non-urgent assessment if there is a lack of progress in primary care, despite the above measures.

If available, consider family therapy for anorexic patients (under 18 years),[103] individual psychotherapy for anorexic patients over 18, and cognitive behavioural therapy[104] for those with bulimia.

Consider non-statutory/voluntary services/self-help groups.

Resources for patients and families

Resource leaflets: 9–1 *Food and behaviour diary* and 9–2 *Monitoring and delaying binges*.

Eating Disorders Association   01603 621 414 (helpline 9 am–6.30 pm)
(Self-help support groups for sufferers, their relatives and friends. Assists in putting people in touch with sources of help in their own area)

Centre for Eating Disorders (Scotland)   0131 668 3051
(Information, private psychotherapy, self help manuals, information packs, helpline)

Anorexia Bulimia Careline (Northern Ireland)   02890 614440

Overeaters Anonymous   01454 857158 (recorded message)
(Self-help groups for those suffering from eating disorders or overeating)

Getting Better Bit(e) by Bit(e) by Ulrike Schmidt and Janet Treasure. Lawrence Erlbaum Associates Ltd, 1993
(A self-help manual of proven efficacy for sufferers of bulimia and binge-eating disorders)[105]

Overcoming Binge Eating by Christopher Fairburn. Guildford Press, 1995
(Advice tested in controlled research.)

Generalized anxiety — F41.1

Presenting complaints

The patient may present initially with tension-related physical symptoms (eg headache or a pounding heart) or with insomnia. Enquiry will reveal prominent anxiety.

Diagnostic features

Multiple symptoms of anxiety or tension include:

- physical arousal (eg dizziness, sweating, a fast or pounding heart, a dry mouth, stomach pains, or chest pains)
- mental tension (eg worry, feeling tense or nervous, poor concentration, fear that something dangerous will happen and the patient won't be able to cope)
- physical tension (eg restlessness, headaches, tremors, or an inability to relax).

Symptoms may last for months and recur regularly. Often, they are often triggered by stressful events in those prone to worry.

Differential diagnosis

- **Depression — F32#** (if low or sad mood is prominent).
- **Chronic mixed anxiety and depression — F41.2**.
- **Panic disorder — F41.0** (if discrete attacks of unprovoked anxiety are present).
- **Phobic disorders— F40** (if fear and avoidance of specific situations are present).
- **Alcohol misuse — F10** or **Drug-use disorders —F11#** (if heavy alcohol or drug use is present).
- Certain physical conditions (eg thyrotoxicosis) or medications (eg methylxanthines and beta agonists) may cause anxiety symptoms.
- Anxiety can be a symptom of **Post-traumatic stress disorder — F43.1**.

Essential information for patient and family

- Stress and worry have both physical and mental effects.
- Learning skills to reduce the effects of stress (not sedative medication) is the most effective relief.[106]

Advice and support to patient and family

- Encourage the patient to use relaxation methods daily to reduce physical symptoms of tension. (R: 1–2) ▄
- Advise reduction in caffeine consumption.[46]
- Avoid using alcohol or cigarettes to cope with anxiety.
- Encourage the patient to engage in pleasurable activities and to resume activities that have been helpful in the past.
- Identify and challenge exaggerated worries to help patient reduce anxiety symptoms:
  - Identify exaggerated worries or pessimistic thoughts (eg when daughter is five minutes late from school, patient worries that she may have had an accident).
  - Discuss ways to question these exaggerated worries when they occur (eg when the patient starts to worry about the daughter, the patient could tell him/herself, 'I am starting to be caught up in worry again. My daughter is only a few minutes late and should be home soon. I won't call the school to check unless she's an hour late'. (R: 4–2) ▄
- Identify practice or non-statutory resources for problem-solving, relaxation, yoga.
- Regular physical exercise is often helpful.
- Structured problem-solving methods[48] can help patients to manage current life problems or stresses which contribute to anxiety symptoms. (R: 1–1) ▄
  - Identify events that trigger excessive worry. (For example, a young woman presents with worry, tension, nausea and insomnia. These symptoms began after her son was diagnosed with asthma. Her anxiety worsens when he has asthmatic episodes.)
  - List as many possible solutions as the patient can think of (eg meeting with the nurse to learn about asthma management, discussing her concerns with other parents of asthmatic children, writing down a management plan for asthma episodes).
  - List the advantages and disadvantages of each possible solution. (The patient should do this, perhaps between appointments.)
  - Support the patient in choosing his or her preferred approach.

— Help the patient to work out the steps necessary to achieve the plan.
— Set a date to review the plan. Identify and reinforce things that are working.

Medication

Medication is a secondary treatment in the management of generalized anxiety.[106,107] It may be used, however, if significant anxiety symptoms persists despite the measures suggested above.

Anti-anxiety medication[N108] (see BNF section 4.1.2) may be used for no longer than *two weeks*. Avoid short-acting benzodiazepines; consider diazepam. Longer-term use may lead to dependence, and is likely to result in the return of symptoms when discontinued.

Antidepressant drugs,[109] for example imipramine, clomipramine, paroxetine or venlafaxine, may be helpful (especially if symptoms of depression are present). They do not lead to dependence or rebound symptoms, but can lead to withdrawal symptoms and so should be tapered gradually. (See BNF section 4.3.)

• Beta-blockers may help control physical symptoms such as tremor.[110]

Referral

See general referral criteria.

Non-urgent referral to secondary mental-health services is advised if the patient's symptoms are sufficiently severe or enduring to interfere with his/her social or occupational functioning.

If available, consider cognitive/behavioural therapy or anxiety management.[N111] Self-care classes and 'assisted bibliotherapy' can also be effective in primary care for milder anxiety.[112,113]

Resources for patients and families

Resource leaflets: 1–1 *Problem solving*, 1–2 *Learning to relax*, 4–1 *Anxiety and how to reduce it* and 4–2 *Dealing with anxious thoughts*.

No Panic   01952 590545 (10 am–10 pm helpline)
(Helpline, information booklets and local self-help groups for people with anxiety, phobias obsessions, panic)

Who's afraid ...? Coping with fear, anxiety and panic attacks by Alice Neville, Arrow Books, 1991

Mind Publications produces booklets on *Understanding anxiety* and other relevant topics.

Mind England: 020 8519 2122; **Northern Ireland:** 02890 237937; **Scotland:** 0141 568 7000

Triumph Over Phobia (TOP) UK   01225 330353
(Structured self-help groups. Produces self-help materials)

Stresswatch Scotland   01563 574144 (office) 01563 528910 (helpline)
(Advice, information, materials on panic, anxiety, stress phobias; 35 local groups)

Yoga and meditation classes available in adult education programmes at most Colleges of Further Education.

Panic disorder — F41.0

Presenting complaints

Patients may present with one or more physical symptoms (eg chest pain, dizziness or shortness of breath) or unexplained episodes of intense fear. Further enquiry shows the full pattern described below.

Diagnostic features

The patient experiences unexplained attacks of anxiety or fear, which begin suddenly, develop rapidly and may last only a few minutes.

The panics often occur with physical sensations such as palpitations, chest pain, sensations of choking, churning stomach, dizziness, feelings of unreality, or fear of personal disaster (losing control or going mad, sudden death or having a heart attack).

A panic often leads to fear of another panic attack and avoidance of places where panics have occurred.

Differential diagnosis

Many medical conditions may cause symptoms similar to panic (eg arrhythmia, cerebral ischaemia, coronary disease, asthma or thyrotoxicosis). It is not uncommon for individuals with these conditions to additionally suffer from panic. History and physical examination should exclude many of these and should reassure the patient. However, avoid unnecessary medical tests or therapies

- Drugs may induce symptoms of panic.
- **Phobic disorders — F40** (if panics tend to occur in specific situations).
- **Depression — F32#** (if low or sad mood is also present).

Essential information for patient and family

- Panic is common and can be treated.

- Anxiety often produces frightening physical symptoms. Chest pain, dizziness or shortness of breath are not necessarily signs of a physical illness; they will pass when anxiety is controlled. Explain how the body's arousal reaction provides the physical basis for their symptoms and how anxiety about a physical symptom can create a vicious cycle. A diagram may be helpful.

- Panic anxiety also causes frightening thoughts (eg fear of dying, a feeling that one is going mad or will lose control) and *vice versa*. These also pass when anxiety is controlled.

- Mental and physical anxiety reinforce each other. Concentrating on physical symptoms will increase fear.

- A person who withdraws from or avoids situations where panics have occurred will only strengthen his/her anxiety.

Advice and support to patient and family[N106]

- Advise the patient to identify the early warning signs of an impending panic attack and take the following steps at the first sign of panic:
  - Stay where you are until the panic passes, which may take up to an hour. Do NOT leave the situation. Start slow, relaxed breathing, counting up to four on each breath in and each breath out. Breathing too deeply (hyperventilation) can cause some of the physical symptoms of panic. Controlled breathing will reduce physical symptoms. Do something to focus your thinking on something visible, tangible and non-threatening (eg look at the books in the supermarket).
  - If hyperventilation is severe, sit down and breath into a paper bag so that the increased carbon dioxide will slow down your breathing (unless the patient has asthma or cardiovascular disease).
  - Concentrate on controlling anxiety and not on the physical symptoms.
  - Tell yourself that this is a panic attack and that frightening thoughts and sensations will eventually pass. Note the time passing on your watch. It may feel like a long time but it will usually only be a few minutes.

- Identify exaggerated fears that occur during panic (eg patient's fear that he/she is having a heart attack).

- Discuss ways to challenge these fears during panic (eg the patient could remind him/herself, 'I am not having a heart attack. This is a panic, and it will pass in a few minutes').

- Monitor and, if necessary, reduce caffeine intake.

- Avoid using alcohol or cigarettes to cope with anxiety.
- Self-help groups, books, tapes or leaflets may help the patient manage panic symptoms and overcome fears.[114]
  (R: 4–1, 4–2) 💾

Medication

Many patients will benefit from the above measures and will not need medication, unless their mood is low.

- If attacks are frequent and severe, or if the patient is significantly depressed, antidepressants, including tricyclics and SSRIs, may be helpful.[N115] Paroxetine and citalopram are currently licenced for panic (see BNF section 4.3). There can be a slight worsening of symptoms initially, so advise the patient to plan reduced activities for the week following the first prescription.
- Encourage patients to face fears without use of benzodiazepines or alcohol. However, where the feared situation is rare (eg flying, for someone who flies rarely), occasional, short-term use of anti-anxiety medication may be helpful.[N116] Regular use may lead to dependence and is likely to result in return of symptoms when discontinued. Some patients may find it helpful to have some tablets to use in a future situation.

Referral

See general referral criteria.

Non-urgent referral to secondary mental-health services or practice counsellor with appropriate special training is advised for assessment for cognitive behavioural psychotherapy for patients who do not improve or those whose lifestyle is severely compromised. (This can be particularly effective for patients with panic disorder.[117,118]) CBT treatment, which has been developed in specialist settings, also appears to be effective in primary care.[119]

Panic commonly causes physical symptoms; avoid unnecessary medical referral for physical symptoms if certain of the diagnosis.

Consider self-help/voluntary/non-statutory services.

Resources for patients and families

Resource leaflets: 4–1 *Anxiety and how to reduce it*, 4–2 *Dealing with anxious thoughts*, 1–1 *Problem-solving* and 1–2 *Learning to relax*.

No Panic   01952 590545 (10 am–10 pm helpline)
(Helpline, information booklets and local self help groups for people with anxiety, phobias, obsessions and panic)
Who's afraid ...? Coping with fear, anxiety and panic attacks by Alice Neville, Arrow Books, 1991

Mind   Publications produces booklets on *How to cope with panic attacks* and other relevant topics

Mind   England: 020 8519 2122. Northern Ireland: 02890 237937. Scotland: 0141 568 7000

Triumph Over Phobia (TOP) UK   01225 330353
(Structured self-help groups. Produces self-help materials)

Stresswatch Scotland   01563 574144 (office) 01563 528910 (helpline)
(Advice, information and materials on panic, anxiety, stress phobias. 35 local groups)

Living with fear by Isaac Marks. McGraw Hill. Self-help manual.

Phobic disorders — F40 (includes agoraphobia and social phobia)

Presenting complaints

Patients may avoid or restrict activities because of fear. They may have difficulty travelling to the doctor's surgery, going shopping or visiting others. This may lead to unemployment and social or financial problems.

Patients sometimes present with physical symptoms (eg palpitations, shortness of breath or 'asthma'). Questioning will reveal specific fears.

Diagnostic features

The patient experiences an unreasonably strong fear of people, specific places or events. Patients often avoid these situations altogether.

Commonly feared situations include:

- leaving home
- open spaces
- speaking in public
- crowds or public places
- travelling in buses, cars, trains or planes
- social events.

Patients may avoid leaving home or being alone because of fear.

Differential diagnosis

- **Panic disorder — F41.0** (if anxiety attacks are prominent and not brought on by anything in particular).
- **Depression— F32#** (if low or sad mood is prominent).

Panic disorder and depression may co-exist with phobias.

Many of the guidelines below also may be helpful for specific (simple) phobias (eg fear of water or heights).

Essential information for patient and family

- Phobias can be treated successfully.
- Avoiding feared situations allows the fear to grow stronger.
- Following certain steps can help someone overcome fear.

Advice and support to patient and family[N106] (R: 4–1, 4–2, 4–3) 🖫

- Assess the patient's understanding of the problem and readiness to change.

79

- Encourage the patient to practise controlled breathing methods to reduce physical symptoms of fear. See advice on '**Panic disorders — F41.0**'.
- Ask the patient to make a list of all situations that he/she fears and avoids although other people do not.
- Discuss ways to challenge these exaggerated fears (eg patient reminds him/herself, 'I am feeling anxious because there is a large crowd. The feeling will pass in a few minutes').
- Help the patient to plan a series of progressively more challenging steps whereby the patient confronts and gets used to feared situations. (R: 4-3)▛
  - Identify a small, first step toward the feared situation (eg if afraid of leaving home, take a short walk away from home with a family member).
  - Practise this step for one hour each day until it is no longer frightening.
  - If entering the feared situation still causes anxiety, carry out slow and relaxed breathing, saying the panic will pass within 30–60 min. See advice on '**Panic disorder — F41.0**'.
  - Do not leave the feared situation until the fear subsides. Do not move onto the next step until the current situation is mastered.
  - Move on to a slightly more difficult step and repeat the procedure (eg spend a longer time away from home; then do this alone).
  - Take no alcohol or anti-anxiety medicine for at least four hours before practising these steps.
- Ask a friend or family member to help plan exercises to overcome the fear (R: 4–4)▛. Self-help groups can assist in confronting feared situations.
- Keep a diary of the confrontation experiences described above, to allow step-by-step management.
- Avoid using alcohol or benzodiazepines to cope with feared situations.

Medication
With use of these behavioural methods, many patients will not need medication.[N106]

- If depression is also present, antidepressant medication may be indicated. Paroxetine may be helpful in social phobia.[N120] (See BNF section 4.3.3.)
- Encourage patients to face fears without use of benzodiazepines or alcohol. However, where the feared situation is rare,

however (eg flying, for someone who flies rarely), occasional, short-term use of anti-anxiety medication may be helpful.[N116] Regular use may lead to dependence and is likely to result in return of symptoms when discontinued. Some patients may find it helpful to have some tablets to use in a future situation.

- For management of performance anxiety (eg fear of public speaking), beta-blockers may reduce physical symptoms.[110]

Referral

See general referral criteria.

Non-urgent referral to secondary mental-health services is advised:

- if disabling fears persist (eg the patient is unable to leave home)
- to prevent problems with long-term sickness and disability

If available, cognitive behavioural psychotherapy and exposure[121] may be effective for patients who do not improve with simple measures outlined above.

Recommend self-help/non-statutory/voluntary services (eg Triumph Over Phobia) in all other cases where symptoms persist.

Resources for patients and families

Resource leaflets: 4–1 *Anxiety and how to reduce it*, 4.2 *Dealing with anxious thoughts*, 4–3 *How to overcome a phobia* and 4.4 *Helping someone else to overcome a phobia*.

Triumph Over Phobia (TOP UK)   01225 330353
(Structured self-help groups for those suffering from phobias or obsessive compulsive disorder. Produces self-help materials)

Stresswatch Scotland   01563 574144 (office) 01563 528910 (helpline)
(Advice, information and materials on panic, anxiety, stress phobias. 35 local groups)

Living with fear by Dr Isaac Marks. McGraw Hill. (Self-help manual).

Post-traumatic stress disorder — F43.1

Presenting complaints

The patient may present initially with:

- irritability
- memory and/or concentration problems
- associated difficulties in interpersonal relationships
- impaired occupational functioning
- low mood
- loss of interest
- physical problems

Presentation may be delayed for several months following the trauma.

Diagnostic features

- History of a stressful event or situation (either short- or long-lasting) of an exceptionally threatening or catastrophic nature, which is likely to cause pervasive distress to almost anyone. The trigger event may have resulted in death or injury and/or the patient may have experienced intense horror, fear or helplessness.
- Intrusive symptoms: memories, flashbacks and nightmares
- Avoidance symptoms: avoidance of thoughts, activities, situations and cues reminiscent of the trauma, with a sense of 'numbness', emotional blunting, detachment from other people, unresponsiveness to surroundings or anhedonia.
- Symptoms of autonomic arousal (eg hypervigilance, increased startle reaction, insomnia, irritability, excessive anger, and impaired concentration and/or memory).
- Symptoms of anxiety and/or depression.
- Drug and/or alcohol abuse are commonly associated with this condition.
- Significant functional impairment.

Differential diagnosis

- **Depression** — F32# (if preoccupation with, and ruminations about, a past traumatic event have emerged during a depressive episode).

- **Phobic disorders — F40** (if the patient avoids specific situations or activities after a traumatic event, but has no re-experiencing symptoms).
- Obsessive compulsive disorder (if recurrent, intrusive thoughts or images occur in the absence of an event of exceptionally threatening or catastrophic nature).

Essential information for the patient and family

- Traumatic or life-threatening events often have psychological effects. For the majority, symptoms will subside with minimal intervention. (R: 2) 📖
- For those who continue to experience symptoms, effective treatments are available.
- Suffering from post-traumatic stress disorder is not a weakness and does not mean the patient has gone 'mad'. The patient needs support and understanding, not to be told to 'snap out of it'.

Advice and support to patient and family

- Educate the patient and family about post-traumatic stress disorder, thus helping them understand the patient's changes in attitude and behaviour.
- Avoiding discussion about the event that triggered this condition is unhelpful. Encourage the patient to talk about it.
- Explain the role of avoidance of cues associated with the trauma in reinforcing and maintaining fears and distress. Encourage the patient to face avoided activities and situations gradually.
- Ask about suicide risk, particularly if marked depression is present.
- Avoid using alcohol or cigarettes to cope with anxiety.

Medication

- Consider antidepressant for concurrent depressive illness. See 'Depression — F32#'.
- Antidepressant medication, including tricyclics and SSRIs, may be useful for the treatment of intrusion and avoidance symptoms[N122] (see BNF section 4.3). Drug treatments for this condition generally need to be used in higher doses and for longer periods than those used for treating depression. There may be a latent period of eight weeks or more before the effects are seen.
- Startle and hyperarousal symptoms may be helped by beta-blockers[N122] (see BNF section 2.4).

Referral

See general referral criteria.

Referral to secondary mental-health services is advised if the patient is still having severe intrusive experiences and avoidance symptoms, and there is marked functional disability despite the above measues. If available, consider behaviour therapy (exposure) or cognitive techniques.[N123,N124]

Resources for patients and their families

Medical Foundation for the Care of Victims of Torture
020 7482 0219
(Provides survivors of torture with medical treatment, social assistance and psychotherapeutic support

CombatStress   020 8543 6333
Scottish Office 01292 560 214/724, Irish Office 02890 230329
(Formerly known as the 'Ex-services Mental Welfare Association', it supports men and women discharged from the armed services and Merchant Navy who suffer from mental health problems, including post-traumatic stress disorder. It has a regional network of welfare officers who visit people at home or in hospital. They give some practical and financial help)

Trauma Aftercare Trust (TACT)   01242 890498 (24-hr helpline)
(Provides information about counselling and treatment)

Refugee Support Centre   020 7820 3606
(Provides counselling to refugees, aylum seekers; plus training and information to health and social care professionals on psycho-social needs of refugees)

Victim Support   020 7735 9166; 0845 30 30 900 (Supportline, 9 am–9 pm, Monday–Friday; 9 am–7 pm, Saturday and Sunday; 9 am–5 pm, Bank holidays)
(Emotional and practical support for victims of crime).

Sexual disorders (female) — F52

Presenting complaints

Patients may be reluctant to discuss sexual matters. They may instead complain of physical symptoms, depressed mood or relationship problems. There may have been sexual abuse — in childhood or later.

Special problems may occur in cultural minorities.

Patients may present sexual problems during a routine cervical-smear test.

Diagnostic features

Common sexual disorders presenting in women are:

- lack or loss of sexual desire, arousal or enjoyment
- vaginismus or spasmodic contraction of vaginal muscles on attempted penetration
- dyspareunia (pain in the vagina or pelvic region during intercourse)
- anorgasmia (inability to experience orgasm or climax).

Differential diagnosis

- If low or sad mood is prominent, see 'Depression — F32#'. Depression may cause low desire, or may result from sexual and relationship problems.
- Relationship problems. Where there is persistent discord in the relationship, relationship counselling should precede or accompany specific treatment of the sexual dysfunction.
- Gynaecological disorders (eg vaginal infections, pelvic infections [salpingitis] and other pelvic lesions [leg tumours or cysts], although vaginismus rarely has a physical cause).
- Side-effects of medication, alcohol or drugs (eg SSRI antidepressants, oral contraceptives and beta-blockers).
- Physical illnesses may contribute (eg multiple sclerosis, diabetes or spinal injury).

LACK OR LOSS OF SEXUAL DESIRE

Essential information for patient and partner

The level of sexual desire varies widely between Individuals. Loss of or low sexual desire has many causes, including relationship

85

problems, earlier traumas, fear of pregnancy, post-natal problems, physical and psychiatric illnesses and stress. The problem can be temporary or persistent.

Advice and support to patients and partner

Discuss patient's beliefs about sexual relations. Check whether the patient and/or the partner has unreasonably high expectations. Ask the patient about traumatic sexual experiences and negative attitudes to sex. Accept that this may take more than one appointment. If possible, see partners together, as well as individually. Suggest planning sexual activity for specific days. Suggest ways of building self-esteem (eg exercise or education) and advise time and space to herself.

VAGINISMUS

Essential information for patient and partner

Vaginismus is an involuntary spasm of the pubococcygeal muscles, accompanied by intense fear of penetration and anticipation of pain and usually caused by psychosocial factors (eg previous negative sexual experiences). It can be overcome with specific psychosexual therapy.

Advice and support to patient and partner

Exercises are recommended for the patient, and later on, partner, with graded dilators or finger dilation, accompanied by Kegel exercises, relaxation exercises, treatment for anxiety and couple counselling. Treatment often requires intensive therapy but has a promising outcome.

DYSPAREUNIA

Essential information for patient and partner

There are many physical causes, both of deep and superficial dyspareunia. In some cases, however, anxiety, poor lubrication and muscle tension are the main factors. Even where there has been a physical cause and it has resolved, anticipation of pain may frequently maintain the dyspareunia.

Advice and support to patient and partner

Check if patient experiences desire/arousal/lubrication. Relaxation, prolonged foreplay and careful penetration may overcome psychogenic problems. Referral to a gynaecologist or GUM clinic is advisable if simple measures are unsuccessful.

Essential information for patient and spouse

Many women are unable to experience orgasm during intercourse but can often achieve it by clitoral stimulation.

Advice and support to patient and partner

Discuss the couple's beliefs and attitudes. Encourage self-pleasuring, manually or using a vibrator. The couple should be helped to communicate openly and to reduce any unrealistic expectations. Books, leaflets or educational videos may be useful (see 'Resources for patients and their families' below).

Referral

Patients can refer themselves to:

- Relate
- Brook Advisory Centres
- Family planning clinics
- Genito-urinary medicine clinics

Consider referral to a psychosexual specialist if patient and doctor are unable to enter into a programme of treatment or if primary-care treatment has failed.

Resources for patients and their families

Relate   01788 573241
(Relationship counselling for couples or individuals over aged 16. Sex therapy for couples. Clients pay on a sliding scale)

Brook Advisory Centres   020 7617 8000 (24-hr helpline)
(Free counselling and confidential advice on contraception and sexual matters especially for young people [under 25])

Becoming orgasmic: a sexual growth program for women by Heiman and LoPiccolo. Prentice-Hall, 1988 (Self-help exercises for anorgasmia)

Treat yourself to sex by Brown and Faulder. Penguin Books, 1977

A woman's guide to overcoming sexual fear and pain by Goodwin and Agronin. New Harbinger Publishers, 1997.

Sexual disorders (male) — F52

Presenting complaints

Patients may be reluctant to discuss sexual matters. They may instead complain of physical symptoms, depressed mood or relationship problems.

Special problems may occur in different cultures. Sexual problems are often somatized, expectations may be high, and psychological explanations and therapies may not be readily accepted.

Diagnostic features

Common sexual disorders presenting in men are:

- erectile dysfunction or impotence
- premature ejaculation
- retarded ejaculation or orgasmic dysfunction (intravaginal ejaculation is greatly delayed or absent but can often occur normally during masturbation
- lack or loss of sexual desire.

Differential diagnosis

- **Depression** — F32# (if low or sad mood is prominent).
- Problems in relationships with partners often contribute to sexual disorder, especially those of desire. Where there is persistent discord in the relationship, relationship counselling should precede or accompany specific treatment of the sexual dysfunction.
- Specific organic pathology is a rare cause of orgasmic dysfunction or premature ejaculation.
- Physical factors which may contribute to erectile dysfunction include diabetes, hypertension, alcohol abuse, smoking, medication (eg antidepressants, antipsychotics, diuretics and beta-blockers), multiple sclerosis and spinal injury.
- Patients may have unreasonable expectations of their own performance.

ERECTILE DYSFUNCTION (FAILURE OF GENITAL RESPONSE, IMPOTENCE)

Essential information for patient and partner

Erectile dysfunction is often a temporary response to stress or loss of confidence and responds to psychosexual treatment especially if morning erections occur. It may also be caused by physical factors (neurological or vascular), by medication, or may be secondary to the ageing process.

Advice and support to patient and partner

Advise patient and partner to refrain from attempting intercourse for two to three weeks. Encourage them to practise pleasurable physical contact without intercourse during that time, commencing with non-genital touching and moving through mutual genital stimulation to a gradual return to full intercourse at the end of that period. Progression along this continuum should be guided by the return of consistent, reliable erections. A book containing self-help exercises (see 'Resources for patients and their families' below) may be helpful. Inform patient and partner of the possibilities of physical treatment by penile rings, vacuum devices, intracavernosal injections and medication.

Medication

- Oral: Sildenafil 50–100 mg taken on an empty stomach 40–60 min before intercourse enhances erections in 80% of patients, whether the cause is psychogenic or neurological.[125] Beware danger of interaction with cardiac nitrates (see BNF section 7.4.5)
- Intraurethral: MUSE (prostaglandin E_1) 125–1000 µg inserted 10 min before intercourse produces erections in 40–50% of patients[126] (see BNF section 7.4.5).
- Intracavernosal: Prostaglandin E_1 5–20 µg injected 10 min before intercourse produces erections in 80–90% of patients,[127] but long-term acceptability is low.

These medications are less effective in predominantly vasculogenic cases.

See current NHS Executive guidelines for prescription of the above, either privately or on the NHS.

PREMATURE EJACULATION

Essential information for patient and partner

Control of ejaculation is possible and can enhance sexual pleasure for both partners.

Advice and support to patient and partner

Reassure the patient that ejaculation can be delayed by learning new approaches (eg the squeeze or stop–start technique). This, and other exercises, are set out in self-help books (see 'Resources for patients and their families' below). Delay can also, in some cases, be achieved with clomipramine or SSRI medication but relapse is very common on cessation. Local anaesthetic sprays, if used cautiously, can delay ejaculation.

ORGASMIC DYSFUNCTION OR RETARDED EJACULATION

Essential information for patient and partner

This is a more difficult condition to treat; however, if ejaculation can be brought about in some way (eg through masturbation) the prognosis is better. Individual psychotherapy may be required.

Advice and support to patient and partner

Recommend exercises, such as penile stimulation with body oil or masturbation close to the point of orgasm, followed by vaginal penetration.

LACK OR LOSS OF SEXUAL DESIRE

Essential information for patient and partner

The level of sexual desire varies widely between individuals. Lack or loss of sexual desire has many causes, including physical and psychiatric illnesses, stress and relationship problems and rarely, hormonal deficiences. It may merely represent different expectations.

Advice and support to patient and partner

Encourage relaxation, stress reduction, open communication, appropriate assertiveness and cooperation between partners. Educational leaflets, books or videos may be helpful.

Referral

Patients can refer themselves to:

- Relate
- Family planning clinics
- Genito-urinary medicine clinics.

Consider referral if patient and doctor are unable to enter into programme of treatment or if primary-care treatment has failed:

- to a urologist for erectile dysfunction, if unresponsive to medication and counselling
- to a psychosexual specialist, if problem is predominantly psychogenic.

Resources for patients and their families

Relate   01788 573241
(Relationship counselling for couples or individuals over 16.
Sex therapy for couples. Clients pay on a sliding scale)

Brook Advisory Centres   020 7617 8000 (24-hr helpline)
(Free counselling and confidential advice on contraception and
sexual matters especially for young people [under 25])
Men and sex by B Zilbergeld. Fontana, 1980. (Self-help exercises
for erectile dysfunction and premature ejaculation)

Sexual happiness by M Yaffe and E Fenwick. Dorling
Kindersley, 1986.

Sleep problems (insomnia) — F51

Presenting complaints

Patients are distressed by persistent insomnia and are sometimes disabled by the daytime effects of poor sleep (eg driving).

Diagnostic features

- Difficulty falling asleep
- Restless or unrefreshing sleep
- Frequent or prolonged periods of being awake.

Differential diagnosis

- Short-term sleep problems may result from stressful life events, acute physical illnesses or changes in schedule.
- Persistent sleep problems may indicate another cause, for example:
  — **Depression — F32#** (if low or sad mood and loss of interest in activities are prominent)
  — **Generalized anxiety — F41.1** (if daytime anxiety is prominent).

Sleep problems can be a presenting complaint of **Alcohol misuse — F10** or **Substance abuse — F11#**. Enquire about current substance use.

- Consider medical conditions which may cause insomnia (eg heart failure, pulmonary disease and pain conditions).
- Consider medications which may cause insomnia (eg steroids, theophylline, decongestants and some antidepressant drugs).
- If the patient snores loudly while asleep, consider sleep apnoea. It will be helpful to take a history from the bed partner. Patients with sleep apnoea often complain of daytime sleepiness but are unaware of night-time awakenings.

Essential information for patient and family

- Temporary sleep problems are common at times of stress or physical illness.
- Sleep requirements vary widely and usually decrease with age.
- Improvement of sleeping habits (not sedative medication) is the best treatment.[128]
- Worry about not being able to sleep can worsen insomnia.

- Alcohol may help a person to fall asleep but can lead to restless sleep and early awakening.
- Stimulants (including coffee and tea) can cause or worsen insomnia.

Advice and support to patient and family

- Encourage the patient to maintain a regular sleep routine by:
  — relaxing in the evening
  — keeping to regular hours for going to bed and getting up in the morning, trying not to vary the schedule or 'sleep in' on the weekend
  — getting up at the regular time even if the previous night's sleep was poor
  — avoiding daytime naps since they can disturb the next night's sleep.
- Daytime exercise can help the patient to sleep regularly, but evening exercise may contribute to insomnia.
- Simple measures may help (eg a milk drink or a hot bath).
- Recommend relaxation exercises to help the patient to fall asleep. (R: 1–2)
- Advise the patient to avoid caffeine and alcohol in the evenings.
- If the patient cannot fall asleep within 30 min, advise him/her to get up and try again later when feeling sleepy.
- Self-help leaflets and books may be useful. (R: 11)
- Sleep diaries are often useful in assessment and monitoring of progress. (R: 11)

Medication

- Treat underlying psychiatric or physical conditions.
- Make changes to medication, as appropriate.
- Hypnotic medication may be used intermittently.[129] Risk of dependence increases significantly after 14 days of use. Avoid hypnotic medication in cases of chronic insomnia (where insomnia is experienced for most nights over at least three weeks.).
- Valerian may have a weak effect on sleep but without a hangover effect the next day.[130]

Referral

See general referral criteria.

Referral to secondary mental-health services is rarely helpful.

Refer to a sleep laboratory, if available, if more complex sleep disorders (eg narcolepsy, night terrors or somnambulism) are suspected.

Where symptoms are severe and long-lasting and the above measures are unsuccessful, consider referral to a clinical psychologist or specially trained counsellor, if available, for therapies such as sleep hygiene training.[N131,132]

Resources for patients and families

Resource leaflets: 1–2 *Learning to relax*, 11 *Overcoming sleep problems* (includes *Sleep diary* on page 5).

Unexplained somatic complaints — F45

Presenting complaints
- Any physical symptom may be present.
- Symptoms may vary widely across cultures.
- Complaints may be single or multiple and may change over time.

Diagnostic features
- Medically unexplained physical symptoms. (A full history and physical examination are necessary to determine this.)
- Frequent medical visits in spite of negative investigations.
- Symptoms of depression and anxiety are common.

  Some patients may be primarily concerned with obtaining relief from physical symptoms. Others may be worried about having a physical illness and be unable to believe that no physical condition is present (hypochondriasis).

Differential diagnosis
- **Drug use disorders — F11#** (eg seeking narcotics for relief of pain).
- If low or sad mood is prominent, see '**Depression — F32#**'. (People with depression are often unaware of everyday physical aches and pains.)
- **Generalized anxiety disorder — F41.1** (if anxiety symptoms are prominent).
- **Panic disorder — F41.0** (misinterpretation of the somatic signs associated with panic).
- **Chronic mixed anxiety and depression — F41.2**.
- **Acute psychotic disorders — F23** (if strange beliefs about symptoms are present [eg belief that organs are decaying]).
- An organic cause may eventually be discovered for the physical symptoms. Psychological problems can co-exist with physical problems.

Depression, anxiety, alcohol misuse or drug use disorders may co-exist with unexplained somatic complaints.

Essential information for patient and family

- Stress often produces or exacerbates physical symptoms.
- The focus should be on managing the symptoms, not on discovering their cause.
- Cure may not always be possible; the goal should be to live the best life possible even if symptoms continue.

Advice and support to patient and family[133] (R: 12)

- Acknowledge that the patient's physical symptoms are real to the patient.
- Ask about the patient's beliefs (what is causing the symptoms?) and fears (what does he/she fear may happen?)
- Be explicit early on about considering psychological issues. The exclusion of illness and exploration of emotional aspects can happen in parallel. Investigations should have a clear indication. It may be helpful to say to the patient, 'I think this result is going to be normal'.
- Offer appropriate reassurance (eg not all headaches indicate a brain tumour). Advise patients not to focus on medical worries.
- Discuss emotional stresses that were present when the symptoms arose.
- Explain the links between stress and physical symptoms and how a vicious cycle can develop (eg 'stress can cause a tightening of the muscles in the gut. This can lead to the development of abdominal pain or worsening of existing pain. The pain aggravates the tightening of the gut muscles'). A diagram may be helpful.
- Relaxation methods can help relieve symptoms related to tension (such as headache, neck or back pain). (R: 1–2)
- Encourage exercise and enjoyable activities. The patient need not wait until all symptoms are gone before returning to normal routines.
- Treat associated depression, anxiety or alcohol problems.
- For patients with more chronic complaints, time-limited appointments that are regularly scheduled can prevent more frequent, urgent visits.[134]
- Structured problem-solving methods may help patients to manage current life problems or stresses which contribute to symptoms[48] (R: 1–1)
  — Help the patient to identify the problem.
  — List as many possible solutions as the patient can think of.
  — List the advantages and disadvantages of each possible solution. (The patient should do this, perhaps between appointments.)

— Support the patient in choosing his or her preferred approach.
— Help the patient to work out the steps necessary to achieve the plan.
— Set a date to review the plan. Identify and reinforce things that are working.

Medication

Avoid unnecessary diagnostic testing or prescription of new medication for each new symptom. Rationalize polypharmacy.

Where depression is also present, an antidepressant may be indicated. (See '**Depression — F32#**'.)

Low doses of tricyclic antidepressant medication (eg amitriptyline, 50–100 mg a day, or imipramine 20 mg a day) may be helpful in some cases (eg when there is headache, atypical chest pain).[135,136]

Referral

- Patients are best managed in primary health-care settings. Consistency of approach within the practice is essential. Seeing the same person is helpful. Consider referral to a partner for a second opinion. Documenting discussions with colleagues can reduce stress by sharing responsibility within the primary-care team.
- Non-urgent referral to secondary mental-health services is advised on grounds of functional disability, especially inablility to work and duration of symptoms.
- Cognitive behaviour therapy, if available, may help some patients, though willingness of patients to participate is sometimes poor.[N137]
- Refer to a liaison psychiatrist, if available, for those who persist in their belief that they have a physical cause for their symptoms, despite good evidence to the contrary.
- Avoid multiple referrals to medical specialists. Documented discussions with appropriate medical specialists may be helpful from time to time as, in some cases, underlying physical illness eventually emerges.

Resources for patients and families

Resource leaflets: 12 *Unexplained physical complaints*, 1–2 *Learning to relax* and 1–1 *Problem-solving*.

Learning disability* — F70

Presenting complaints

In children:

- delay in usual development (eg sitting up, walking, speaking and toilet training)
- difficulty managing school work, as well as other children, because of learning disabilities
- behavioural problems.

  In adolescents:

- difficulties with peers, leading to social isolation
- inappropriate sexual behaviour
- difficulties making the transition to adulthood.

  In adults:

- difficulties in everyday functioning, requiring extra support (eg cooking and cleaning)
- problems with normal social development and establishing an independent life in adulthood (eg finding work, marriage and child-rearing).

Diagnostic features

- Slow or incomplete mental development resulting in:
  — learning difficulties
  — social adjustment problems.
- The range of severity includes:
  — severe learning disability (usually identified before two years of age; requires help with daily tasks and capable of only simple speech)
  — moderate learning disability (usually identified by age three to five; able to do simple work with support, needs guidance or support in daily activities)
  — mild or borderline learning disability (usually identified during school years; limited in school work, but able to live alone and maintain some form of paid employment).

*May also be known internationally as 'Mental retardation'.

Diagnosis of co-morbid conditions

Learning disability is associated with an increased prevalence of many other disorders. The most common include:

- epilepsy (25% people with learning disability and 50% of those with severe learning disability)
- autism
- hearing impairments (40%)
- visual impairments (40%)
- psychiatric and behavioural disorders (35%)
- hypothyroidism (people with Down's Syndrome)
- dementia (people with Down's Syndrome and those over 50 years of age).

Diagnosis of these conditions may be made harder by unusual presentations of illness. For example, *irritability may be an indication of pain or emotional distress.*

Differential diagnosis

The following may also interfere with performance at school:

- specific learning difficulties (eg dyslexia)
- attention deficit disorder
- motor disorders (eg cerebral palsy etc.)
- sensory problems (eg deafness).

Malnutrition or chronic medical illness may cause developmental delays. Most causes of learning disabilities cannot be treated. The more common, treatable causes of learning disability include hypothyroidism, lead poisoning and some inborn errors of metabolism (eg phenylketonuria).

Essential information for patient and family

- Early training can help a person with learning disability towards self care and independence.
- People with learning disabilities are capable of loving relationships and have the same needs as any other person for love, security, play and friendship, together with clear boundaries and limits on behaviour.

Advice and support to patient and family

- Reward effort. Allow disabled children and adults to function at the highest level of their ability in school, work and the family.
- Advise families that learning and practising skills will be helpful, but that 'miracle cures' do not exist. It is usually impossible to predict, at diagnosis, how a child with learning disability will function as an adult.

- Families may feel conflicting emotions — intense love, disappointment, anger, great loss — and may take time and continuing support to adjust to being the parent of a child with learning disability and to deal with different life stages and transitions (eg leaving school, employment, social life and sexuality, death of parents). It may be helpful to talk things through with someone who has had the same experiences (see 'Resources' below). A transition plan can be requested from Social Services for when the young person leaves school, whether or not the child has a statement of special educational need.
- Inform families that people with a learning disability frequently under-report illnesses. Arranging regular health screening can be useful to actively seek out treatable sensory disorders, depression, obesity, skin infections, diabetes and other conditions. It is valuable to review care also at times of transition (eg school leaving) and at times of family illness.
- Encourage the patient to see the same doctor at every appointment, if possible, in order to build trust and reduce problems in communication. Carers who know the patient well are invaluable as informants.

Medication

- Except in the case of certain physical or psychiatric disorders, medical treatment cannot improve cognitive function.
- Learning disabilities may occur with other disorders that require medical treatment (eg seizures, spasticity, and psychiatric illness such as depression).
- Unnecessary medication should be avoided, and medication reviewed regularly, as side-effects and idiosyncratic reactions are common. People with learning disabilities under-report side-effects, so consideration should be given to pro-active checks (eg blood levels of anti-convulsants).

Treating depression

It is helpful to review social networks and support in addition to other treatment. See '**Depression — F32#**'.

Referral

Referral to the community paediatric team or learning disability services (depending on local arrangements) is advised when the learning disability is first identified, to help plan for education and specialist care. Psychiatrists specialising in learning disability are skilled in investigating and treating epilepsy as well as

psychiatric illness.

Referral for specialist support is also advised:

- following the death of a carer or close relative, as there is increased risk of pathological grief
- where there is significant weight change which persists for longer than one month, to exclude emotional or psychiatric disorder
- where there are significant changes in behaviour which persist for longer than one month.

For further information about learning disability, see *Once a Day* NHS Executive guidelines for primary health-care teams, March 1999.

Resources for patients and families

Mencap   020 7454 0454

Mencap Northern Ireland   02890 6911351
0345 636227 (family advisory service)

Down's Syndrome Association   020 8682 4001
Scope   0800 626216 (helpline)
(Support for people with cerebral palsy [only some of whom have learning disability in addition to their physical disabilities])

ASBAH (The Association for Spina Bifida and Hydrocephalus) 01733 555 988

The National Autistic Society   020 7833 2299
(helpline: 020 7903 3555)

Contact a Family   020 7383 3555
(Works across UK to support families caring for children with any disability. Particularly useful where there is a rare condition)

SPOD (Association to Aid the Sexual and Personal Relationships of People with a Disability)   020 7607 8851

Circles Network   0117 939 3917
(Provides information on setting up circles of friends and circles of support to help people with a learning disability have a more interesting social life)

Benefits Enquiry Line   0800 882200
(For information about the Disability Living Allowance (care component) and Invalid Care Allowance).

The Family Fund   01904 621115
(An independent organization helping families caring for a
child with severe disabilities. May help pay for one-off costs
such as holidays and washing machines)

Depression in people with learning disability   020 7235 2351
(Free leaflet available from Royal College of Psychiatrists)

*Learning disabilities and the family: the young child with a learning
disability*, and *Learning disabilities and the family: the teenager with
a severe learning disability*

Available from the **Mental Health Foundation**   020 7535 7400

Books beyond words is a series of picture-books for adolescents
and adults who cannot read. They may be used by parents,
carers, GPs, nurses and others to help communication about
important topics. Titles include *Feeling blue*, about depression,
Going to the doctor, *Going into hospital*, *When dad died*, *Making
friends* and *Falling in love*. The Royal College of Psychiatrists,
17 Belgrave Square, London SW1X 8PG, UK, £10 each.
020 7235 2351 (ext 146).

Assessment under the Mental Health Act England and Wales 1983 — a basic guide for General Practitioners

General Practitioners can be involved in Mental Health Act assessments in a variety of settings:

- *Hospital*: The patient may have already been admitted informally and is now wanting to leave or is refusing treatment.
- *Home*: The patient may be causing serious concern to family or neighbours. If access is denied, section 135 (warrant to search for and remove patients) may need to be used. This warrant is obtained by an approved social worker (ASW) from a Magistrates' Court.
- *Police station*: As a place of safety (section 136), or after arrest for an offence.

The 1983 Mental Health Act provides the legal framework in England and Wales for compulsory admission and treatment of patients suffering from mental illness.

Use of the Mental Health Act

Compulsory admission for assessment and/or treatment can only occur when:

- there is a mental disorder; *and*
- it is in the interest of the health and/or safety of the patient; *or*
- it is in the interest of the protection of others.

The act allows the compulsory admission of a patient who is very distressed or ill (for example, actively psychotic or manic) solely in order to improve their health, even if they are not thought to be at immediate risk of harming themselves or others. It cannot be used for the compulsory treatment of addictions unless the above criteria are also met.

Mental disorder comprises mental illness, mental impairment, severe mental impairment and psychopathic disorder. In the Act, mental illness is not defined but is a matter for clinical judgement.

103

How to arrange a Mental Health Act assessment

A Mental Health Act assessment is activated by telephoning the duty-approved social worker (ASW) or the duty psychiatrist, depending upon local policy.

He/she will need the following information:

Name, date of birth, address, reason for assessment, previous history, including name of keyworker, next of kin (if known) and past history of violence of self harm (if known).

He/she will need enough information to decide if there is the possibility of an admission under the Mental Health Act, and that the full assessment process is warranted.

If you want to discuss the management of the patient, either telephone the duty ASW or the duty consultant.

The ASW will then take responsibility for coordinating the assessment, bringing relevant papers, ensuring the process complies with the law and arranging for the transport of the patient.

Before the assessment
Information is an important component of the assessment.

- If you can access your records, check for previous history and response to treatment, risk of neglect, violence or self harm, any known contact names.
- If there is a relative or informant, ask about the recent situation, its duration, whether there is any support, whether there have been threats or violence and if the patient is known to carry or have access to weapons.
- Liaise with the ASW about directions, access to premises, where to meet and the need for police attendance.
- It is good practice (because it is safer, communication is better and disruption of the patient is minimized) if the medical assessments take place jointly with the ASW at the same agreed time (although, if this is not possible, they are legally allowed to be five days apart. In any case, the two doctors must discuss their decision).

If the patient is suffering from the short-term effect of drugs, alcohol or sedative medication, discussion should take place about deferring the assessment until a more productive interview can take place.

During the assessment

The team necessary to implement a Section 2 (28 days for assessment) or Section 3 (six months for treatment) is:

- an approved psychiatrist (often the duty consultant or specialist registrar)
- a doctor with prior knowledge of the patient (ideally the GP)
- the ASW.

The GP and others in the primary-care team often have prior knowledge of the patient, including access to records and an existing relationship with the patient and or family, which facilitates the assessment. The psychiatrist may not know the patient, but often contributes clinical experience and expertise. The ASW makes a more comprehensive assessment of the social aspects of the case and advises on the legal issues that may arise during the process. He/she sees that the patient is interviewed 'in a suitable manner'.

The patient is interviewed as comfortably as possible, with the following questions in mind:

- Is there any possible evidence of mental illness?
- Is there a risk to the health or safety of the patient or a danger to others?

If the answer to both of these questions is yes:

- Will the patient consent to informal admission, and if so, is that realistic, based on past experience or aspects of the current interview?
- Are there any community alternatives to admission? For example, giving medication at home, community psychiatric nurse visits, crisis services, day hospitals.

All professionals strive to reach a consensus and *if* the doctors agree to make the medical recommendations for compulsory admission, the social worker makes the application to the admitting hospital managers.

Section 2 is appropriate if there is no previous history, the diagnosis is unclear or no treatment plan is in place.

Section 3 specifies the category of mental disorder and is mainly used for patients already known to the service. If the nearest relative objects to the detention, the application cannot proceed.

Arranging admission

If the decision of the team is to admit the patient, the level of security required should be considered. Arrangements are usually made by the psychiatrist for a bed and the ASW for appropriate transport. The ASW usually accompanies the patient and delivers the section papers in person. He/she is responsible for securing the premises of the patient's home. The ASW informs the patient and next of kin of the decision.

If the patient is not admitted

When the patient is not admitted to hospital, a package of follow-up care needs to be agreed with the patient and next of kin, if appropriate. Arrangements may need to be made to contact mental-health or social work teams during working hours to inform them of the assessment, to make a referral, or both. *You are entitled to submit a claim form* (usually held by the ASW).

This is not intended to be a comprehensive guide to the Mental Health Act. Consultation of the most recent Code of Practice is recommended.

Assessment under the Mental Health (Northern Ireland) Order 1986 — a basic guide for General Practitioners

The 1986 Mental Health (Northern Ireland) Order provides the legal framework in Northern Ireland for compulsory admission and treatment of patients suffering from mental illness. GPs can be involved in Mental Health Order assessments in different settings:

- *Community*: The patient may be causing serious concern to family or neighbours. An application may be made for compulsory hospital admission for seven days, renewable to 14 days for assessment (Article 4). In extreme circumstances, if access is denied, a warrant authorizing a police constable to secure access may need to be used (Article 129). This warrant is obtained by an approved social worker (ASW), other officer of the Health and Social Services Trust or a police constable from a Justice of the Peace. If the constable has to enter the premises, by force or otherwise, he must be accompanied by a medical practitioner (usually a GP), who will administer medical treatment if required.
- *Hospital*: The patient may have been admitted informally and is now wanting to leave or is refusing treatment. An application for assessment involves the patient's own GP (or another practitioner who has previous knowledge of the patient) attending hospital to give the medical recommendation. A doctor on the staff of the hospital in which it is intended that the assessment should be carried out cannot give the recommendation except in a case of urgent necessity.

Use of the Mental Health Order

Compulsory admission for assessment of a patient can only occur when:

- he/she is suffering from a mental disorder of a nature or degree which warrants detention in hospital for assessment (or for assessment followed by medical treatment); *and*
- failure to detain the patient would create a substantial likelihood of serious physical harm to him or herself or to other persons.

Criteria for likelihood of serious physical harm are evidence of one of the following:

- the patient has inflicted, or threatened or attempted to inflict, serious physical harm on him/herself;
- the patient's judgement is so affected that he/she is, *or would soon be,* unable to protect him/herself against serious physical harm and that reasonable provision for his/her protection is not available in the community; *or*
- the patient has behaved violently towards other persons or so behaved such that other persons are placed in reasonable fear of serious physical harm to themselves.

Mental disorder comprises mental illness, mental handicap, severe mental handicap and severe mental impairment. In the Order, mental illness is defined as a 'state of mind which affects a person's thinking, perceiving, emotion or judgment to the extent that he requires care or medical treatment in his own interests or the interests of other persons.'

The Order *cannot be used* for the compulsory treatment of *addictions, personality disorders* or *sexual deviancy,* unless the above criteria are also met.

How to arrange a Mental Health Order assessment

An application for compulsory admission needs to be made by either the nearest relative (on Form 1) or an ASW (Form 2), supported by a medical recommendation (Form 3), usually the patient's own GP or, if not, a doctor who knows the patient personally and is not (except of urgent necessity) on the staff of the receiving hospital. Guidance on who is considered to be the 'nearest relative' under the Order is on the back of Form 1.

A Mental Health Assessment is activated by telephoning the duty-approved social worker. An ASW may be essential (in order to make the application), or highly desirable in order to support and advise the relative who is making the application. The ASW also makes an assessment of the social aspects of the case and provides a social report. Telephone them with the following information: name, date of birth, address, reason for assessment, previous history, including name of keyworker, next of kin (if known) and past history of violence of self harm (if known).

He/she will need enough information to decide if there is the possibility of an admission under the Mental Health Act and that the full assessment process is warranted.

If you want to discuss the management of the patient, either telephone the duty ASW or the duty consultant.

Before the assessment

Information is an important component of the assessment.

- If you can access your records, check for previous history and response to treatment, risk of neglect, violence or self harm, and any known contact names.
- If there is a relative or informant, ask about the recent situation, its duration, whether there is any support, whether there have been threats or violence and if the patient is known to carry or have access to weapons.
- Contact the ASW. An ASW may be essential (in order to make the application) or desirable in order to support and advises the relative who is making the application. Liaise with the ASW about directions, access to premises, where to meet and the need for police attendance.
- Where no ASW is involved, liaise with the nearest relative or other informant about directions, access to premises and need for police attendance, *bring Forms 1 and 3 with you* (available from the Health and Social Security Trust). Arrange police attendance if necessary.
- It is good practice (because it is safer, communication is better and disruption of the patient is minimized) for the professionals involved in the application for admission to be present at the same time (although it may be helpful for each to interview the patient separately). Everyone involved should be aware of the need to provide mutual support. In any case the applicant — whether relative or ASW — must have seen the patient within two days of signing the application and the doctor must examine the patient not less than two days before signing the application.

If the patient is suffering from the short-term effect of drugs, alcohol or sedative medication, discussion should take place about deferring the assessment until a more productive interview can take place.

During the assessment

The team necessary to make an application for compulsory admission is either:

- the nearest relative and a doctor (patient's own GP or a doctor who knows the patient personally); *or*
- an ASW and the patient's own GP or a doctor who knows the patient personally.

Where the nearest relative makes the application, advise them that they can ask for an ASW to consider making the application in their stead (as sometimes making such an application may be detrimental to family relationships). Guidance on who is considered to be the 'nearest relative' under the Order is found on the back of Form 1.

Where an ASW makes the application, he/she must consult the nearest relative, unless this causes unreasonable delay. If the nearest relative objects to the application, the ASW must consult another ASW. Where no ASW is involved, a social worker (not necessarily an approved one) must interview the patient as soon as is practicable and provide a social report to the RMO in the receiving hospital.

The patient is interviewed as comfortably as possible with the following questions in mind:

- Is there any possible evidence of mental illness?
- Is there a substantial risk of serious physical harm to the patient or others?

If the answer to both of these questions is *yes*:

- Will the patient consent to informal admission, and if so, is that realistic, based on past experience or aspects of the current interview?
- Are there any community alternatives to admission? For example giving medication at home, community psychiatric nurse visits, crisis services, day hospitals.

The relatives and, if practicable, other significant informants, are interviewed to find out their views of the patient's needs, and whether, and in what ways, the patient's behaviour is different from his/her normal behaviour.

All parties strive to reach a *consensus*, and *if* the doctor agrees to make the medical recommendation for compulsory admission, the social worker or the nearest relative makes the application to the admitting hospital managers.

The doctor's recommendation must be made on *Form 3* and must include the following information: the grounds, including a clinical description of the mental condition of the patient, for the opinion that the detention is warranted; and the evidence for the opinion that failure to detain the patient would create a substantial likelihood of serious physical harm. Examples of what may be considered in assessing the likelihood of serious physical harm include: uncontrolled over-activity likely to lead to exhaustion, gross and protracted neglect of diet which would lead to malnutrition, gross neglect of hygiene and personal safety which would create a hazard to the patient or others, disinhibited behaviour likely to lead to serious physical harm to the patient, his/her family or other persons. A diagnosis of the specific form of mental disorder is not required

Arranging admission

If the decision of the team is to admit the patient, the level of security required should be considered.

If an ASW is involved, arrangements are usually made by the doctor for a bed and the ASW for appropriate transport, unless an ambulance is required, in which case the doctor arranges this. The ASW usually accompanies the patient and delivers the application papers in person. He/she is responsible for securing the premises of the patient's home. The ASW informs the patient and nearest relative of the decision.

If no ASW is involved, liaise with the receiving hospital about arrangements for the patient's admission, transport to hospital and patient's need for care during removal, including medical and nursing escorts if required. Ensure the premises are secured and inform the patient of the decision. The nearest relative may accompany the patient and deliver the application papers.

The patient must be admitted to hospital within two days from the date on which the medical recommendation was signed, otherwise the authority to detain him or her expires.

If the patient is not admitted

When the patient is not admitted to hospital, a package of follow-up care needs to be agreed with the patient and nearest relative, if appropriate. Arrangements may need to be made to contact mental health or social work teams during working hours to inform them of the assessment and/or to make a referral.

This is not intended to be a comprehensive guide to the Mental Health Order. Consultation of the Code of Practice, the Guide and the Mental Health Order is recommended.

Use of the Mental Health (Scotland) Act 1984 — a basic guide for General Practitioners

The 1984 Mental Health (Scotland) Act provides the legal framework in Scotland for compulsory admission and treatment of patients suffering from mental disorder. GPs can be involved in using the Mental Health Act in a variety of circumstances:

- *Emergency recommendation for detention (Section 24)*: Used where admission is urgently required and use of Section 18 would introduce undesirable delay. Admission under Section 24 allows for a period of 72 hours of assessment. Any doctor can legally make the recommendation, but the consent of a Mental Health Officer (a social worker with special training) or a near relative, must be obtained, wherever practicable.
- *Non-emergency admission for up to six months (Section 18)*: Used where admission is required less urgently (eg where the patient's mental state deteriorates over time). In practice, this is mainly used for patients known to the service. An application is required from a Mental Health Officer (or occasionally the nearest relative) and recommendations from a Section 20-approved doctor (usually a psychiatrist and, where the patient is known to the service, the patient's own consultant psychiatrist) and the GP or another doctor with previous knowledge of the patient.
- *Power of entry (Section 117)*: This may need to be used where a patient with possible mental disorder in the community refuses assessment and help. For example, the patient may be behaving eccentrically, live in very poor conditions, may be ill-treated or neglected by others or alone and unable to care for him/herself. This warrant is obtained by a Mental Health Officer from a Justice of the Peace. It allows a police officer, accompanied by a doctor, to force entry. The person may then be removed to a place of safety with a view to assessment for admission under Section 24.
- *Treatment of a patient who is on leave of absence*: A detained patient may be allowed out of hospital on a 'leave of absence' of up to year. GPs must only prescribe psychiatric medications that are consistent with the agreed treatment plan, set out on Form 9

(where the patient is consenting to treatment) or Form 10 (where the patient is not consenting to treatment). GPs should expect to be told of the conditions of the leave of absence, the circumstances in which the patient is likely to be recalled to hospital and the arrangements in relation to treatment.

Use of the Mental Health Act

Compulsory admission can only occur when:

- there is a mental disorder; *and*
- the patient requires hospital admission in the interest of the health or safety of the patient *or* the protection of others; *and*
- such admission cannot be achieved without compulsory measures.

The Act allows the compulsory admission of a patient who is very distressed or ill (for example, actively psychotic or manic) solely in order to improve their health, even if they are not thought to be at immediate risk of harming themselves or others.

Mental disorder comprises mental illness, mental impairment, severe mental impairment and disorder manifested only by persistent abnormally aggressive or seriously irresponsible conduct. In the Act, mental illness is not defined but is a matter for clinical judgement. Dependence on alcohol or drugs is excluded *per se*, but psychiatric symptoms secondary to drug and alcohol abuse (eg drug-induced paranoid psychosis, Korsakoff psychosis) are included. Mental disorder manifested only by mental impairment or only by abnormally aggressive or seriously irresponsible conduct may be grounds for detention under Section 18 only where treatment in hospital is likely to alleviate or prevent a deterioration in the patient's condition.

Before the assessment

Information is an important component of the assessment.

- If you can access your records, check for previous history and response to treatment, risk of neglect, violence or self harm, and any known contact names.
- If there is a relative or informant, ask about the recent situation, its duration, whether there is any support, whether there have been threats or violence and if the patient is known to carry or have access to weapons.
- Contact the duty Mental Health Officer (MHO). For Section 24, involvement of an MHO is desirable; for Section 18, it is

essential. He/she will need the following information: the name, date of birth, address, reason for assessment, previous history, including name of keyworker, next of kin (if known) and past history of violence of self harm (if known). He/she will need enough information to decide if there is the possibility of an admission under the Mental Health Act

- Liaise with the MHO about directions, access to premises, where to meet and the need for police attendance. It is good practice (because it is safer, communication is better and disruption of the patient is minimized) if the medical assessment(s) take place jointly with the MHO at the same agreed time. For Section 24, only one medical recommendation is needed. For Section 18, two are required; they may be provided up to five days apart.

- If the patient is suffering from the short-term effect of drugs, alcohol or sedative medication, discussion should take place about deferring the assessment until a more productive interview can take place.

- Take copies of Form A (the emergency detention form) with you. If no copies of Form A are available, take practice-headed notepaper.

- If you want to discuss the management of the patient, either telephone the duty MHO or the duty consultant.

During the assessment

The patient is interviewed as comfortably as possible with the following questions in mind:

- Is there any possible evidence of mental disorder?
- Is there a risk to the health or safety of the patient or a danger to others?

If the answer to both of these questions is *yes*:

- Will the patient consent to informal admission, and if so, is that realistic, based on past experience or aspects of the current interview?

- Are there any community alternatives to admission? For example, giving medication at home, community psychiatric nurse visits, crisis services, day hospitals.

For Section 24:

- Seek the consent of the MHO or a near relative. A list of who is considered a 'relative' under the Act can be found on Form A. Being involved in the compulsory admission of a relative to hospital can sometimes damage family relationships; therefore, if it is practicable, advise the relative that there is an alternative (that is, an MHO can perform the consent role). If it is not practicable to seek consent from either an MHO or a near relative, a single doctor's recommendation is sufficient, but the reason for failure to seek consent *must* be explained on the recommendation form. If the relative and MHO refuse consent, compulsory admission cannot go ahead.

- Complete the recommendation on Form A (or on practice-headed notepaper), include full details of your qualifications, a declaration that you have examined the patient at the time of the application, that the patient is subject to a mental disorder, that treatment is necessary in the interests of the health or safety of the patient or the protection of others, reasons why detention is urgently necessary and the use of Section 18 is precluded, and whose consent has been obtained (or reasons why it has not been possible to obtain the consent of an MHO or a near relative). The documentation must be completed on the same day as the patient examination.

For Section 18:

The MHO will normally take responsibility for coordinating the assessment, bringing relevant papers and ensuring the process complies with the law.

The team needed for a Section 18 (six months for treatment) is:

- A Section 20-approved doctor. Where the patient is known to the service, this doctor should be the patient's own consultant psychiatrist.
- The nearest relative or an MHO. The MHO makes a more comprehensive assessment of the social aspects of the case and advises on the legal issues that may arise during the process.)
- A doctor with prior knowledge of the patient (ideally the GP).

All professionals strive to reach a *consensus*, and *if* the two doctors agree to make the medical recommendations for compulsory admission, the MHO makes the application to the Sheriff within seven days. The MHO must make the application even if he/she disagrees with the medical recommendations. The Sheriff may call a hearing, which may involve the attendance of the GP to court.

Arranging admission

If the decision of the team is to admit the patient, the level of security required should be considered.

Discuss with the MHO how the patient is to be managed, including who is to accompany the patient and deliver the section papers, who will secure the premises and who inform the patient and relative of the decision. Liaise with the receiving hospital to ensure a bed is available, to discuss arrangements for the patient's admission, transport to hospital and patient's need for care during removal, including medical and nursing escorts, if required.

Emergency detention is not a 'treatment order' and the patient cannot therefore be forced to accept any form of treatment. However, in emergency circumstances, medication can be given under the common law principle of necessity to control acute symptomatology or behavioural disturbance where risk to life and safety are involved.

If the patient is not admitted

When the patient is not admitted to hospital, a package of follow-up care needs to be agreed with the patient and next of kin, if appropriate. Arrangements may need to be made to contact mental-health or social-work teams during working hours to inform them of the assessment and/or to make a referral.

This is not intended to be a comprehensive guide to the Mental Health Act. Consultation of the most recent Code of Practice is recommended.

Template chart for local resources — statutory services

It is important for clinicians in primary care to have ready access to information about local agencies that can help their patients. The following page contains a suggested template for a simple wall chart. Alternatively, the information can be available on computer in consultations. You may find it helpful to fill in the names and telephone numbers of local agencies, plus the arrangements for referral (for example, what is considered to be an emergency and the standard time to appointment for an urgent referral), enlarge and copy the chart and put it on the walls of all consulting rooms. Set a date for re-checking the telephone numbers and up-dating the charts and delegate this task to a specific person. This could be done on a primary care organization or practice basis.

Local statutory services for mental health and learning disability

	Adults	Elderly	Child and adolescent	Learning disability
Inpatient services				
Community services		Old age psychiatrist Neurologist Community resource team Day care Chiropody Incontinence nurse	Child psychiatric clinic Day unit Child psychotherapy Clinical psychology	Learning disability psychiatric team Occupational therapist Learning disability nurse Child development centre Toy library Physiotherapy Speech therapy Day care
Social services	Adult mental health teams ASW services.	Elderly teams Occupational therapist Elderly mental health services		Adult learning disability social care team Residential care
Department of Social Security				
Agreed priority groups				
Referral arrangements:				
Emergency referrals (9 am–5 pm Mon–Fri)				
Emergency referrals (outside working hours)				
Urgent referrals				
Routine referrals				

Template chart for local resources — voluntary agencies

Non-statutory, voluntary services for mental health and learning disability		
Alcohol/drug support	**Carer support**	**Ethnic support**
Anxiety/stress	**Depression**	**Parents and children**
Learning disability	**Counselling**	**Suicidal thoughts and self harm**
Bereavement	**Elderly support**	**Relationships**
Welfare Citizens Advice Bureau Benefits Agency Debt Counselling	**Mental illness** MIND Manic Depression Fellowship National Schizophrenia Fellowship User support service	**Young people**

This is a suggested template for a simple wall chart. Alternatively, the information can be available on computer in consultations. You may find it helpful to fill in the names and telephone numbers of three local agencies under each heading, enlarge and copy the chart and put it on the walls of all consulting rooms. Set a date for re-checking the telephone numbers and up-dating the charts and delegate this task to a specific person. This could be done on a primary care organization or practice basis.

Resource directory

The following self-help, non-statutory and voluntary organizations are all national organizations, and the numbers are head-office numbers. Many of the agencies have networks of support groups across the country and they will be able to tell you where your nearest group is. All encourage self-referral. You may wish to adapt this directory to include details of your local groups.

Alcohol misuse

Al — Anon Family Groups UK and Eire (local groups)
61 Great Dover Street, London SE1 4YF

24-hr helpline: 020 7403 0888

Understanding and support for families and friends of alcoholics whether still drinking or not.
Alateen for young people 12–20 years affected by others' drinking.

Alcoholics Anoymous (local groups)
PO Box 1, Stonebow House, General Service Office, Stonebow, York YO1 7NJ

01904 644026 Administration

Helplines:
020 7352 3001 / 020 7833 0022 (London)
0141 226 2214 (Scotland)
01907 6255574 (Mid-Wales); 01685 875070 (South Wales); 01639 644871 (Swansea)

Helpline and support groups for men and women trying to achieve and maintain sobriety and help other alcoholics to get sober.

Drinkline
UK helpline: 0800 9178282 (Monday to Friday 11 am–11 pm)
Asian Line: 0990 133 480 (Monday 1–8 pm) Hindi, Urdu, Gujerati and Pujabi

Confidential alcohol counselling and information service.

Northern Ireland Community Addiction Service
40 Elmwood Avenue, Belfast BT9 6AZ

02890 664 434.

Scottish Council on Alcohol
2nd Floor, 166 Buchanan Street, Glasgow G1 2NH

0141 333 9677.

Anxiety, panic and phobias

No Panic (local groups)
93 Brands Farm Way, Telford TF3 2JQ

Helpline: 01952 590545 10 am–10 pm
Head Office: 01952 590005
Information line only: 0800 783 1531
Helpline, information booklets and local self-help groups for
people with anxiety, phobias, obsessions and panic.

Stresswatch Scotland
The Barn, 42 Barnweil Road, Kilmarnock KA1 4JF
01563 574144 (office)
Helpline: 01563 528910 10 am–1 pm Mon–Fri, excluding Wed

Advice, information and materials on panic, anxiety and stress
phobias. 35 local groups.

Triumph Over Phobia (TOP UK) (local groups)
PO Box 1831, Bath BA2 4YW

01225 330353 (office)

Structured self-help groups for those suffering from phobias or
obsessive compulsive disorder. Each group has a volunteer leader
and four or five supporters. Average recovery rate is five months.

Bereavement

Cruse Bereavement Care (local groups)
126 Sheen Road, Richmond, Surrey TW9 1UR

020 8940 4818

National helpline: 0345 585565
Help for bereaved people and those caring for bereaved people.

Foundation for the Study of Infant Deaths (FSID) (local groups)
14 Halkin Street, London SW1X 7DP

020 7235 1721 24-hr helpline
020 7235 0965 (enquiries)

National helpline, local parent groups and befrienders.

Still Birth and Neonatal Death Society (SANDS)
28 Portland Place, London W1N 4DE

020 7436 5881
020 7436 7940 (Admin)

Support for parents whose baby is stillborn or dies within 28 days of birth.

Compassionate Friends
53 North Street, Bristol BS3 1EN

Helpline: 0117 953 9639 9.30 am–5 pm

National organization of bereaved parents offering friendship and understanding to other bereaved parents.

Bipolar disorder (Manic depression)

Manic Depression Fellowship (local groups)
8–10 High Street, Kingston-upon-Thames, Surrey KT1 1EY

020 8974 6550

Advice, support, local self-help groups and publications list for people with manic depressive illness.

Manic Depression Fellowship (Scotland)
7 Woodside Crescent, Glasgow G37UL

0141 331 0344

Carers

Carers National Association (local groups)
20–25 Glasshouse Yard, London EC1A 4JS

020 7490 8818
Helpine: 0808 808 7777 10 am–12 noon and 2 pm–4 pm

Activities include information and advice service for carers.

Association of Crossroads Care Attendants Scheme (local groups)

10 Regent Place, Rugby CV21 2PN

01788 573653

One hundred and ninety regional centres throughout UK, providing practical support and help for carers, including respite care, day centres, befriending and night care. Scheme for young carers also.

Children and adolescents (see also 'Parents and children' below)

Childline

0800 1111 24 hours, free

Confidential helpline for children and young people.

ERIC (Enuresis Resource and Information Centre)

Helpline: 0117 960 3060 (9.30 am–5.30 pm, weekdays)

Information, pen-pal system for children, and details of all enuresis clinics in the country.

Young Minds Trust

102–108 Clerkenwell Road, London EC1 5SA, UK

020 7336 8445
Parent information service: 0800 018 2138

Produces a range of leaflets for parents and young people.

Counselling and psychotherapy

UK Register of Counsellors

01788 568739

Supplies names and addresses of British Association of Counsellors (BAC)-accredited counsellors. They are all appropriately trained and qualified, work to codes of ethics and are subject to complaints procedures.

United Kingdon Council for Psychotherapy (UKCP)
020 7487 7554

Provides information on registered therapists and training organizations.

Counsellors in Primary Care (CPC)
95 Hewarts Lane, Bognor Regis, West Sussex PO21 3DJ

01243 268322

Members are counsellors who work in primary care and who meet defined standards of training and practice.

The British Confederation of Psychotherapists
020 8830 5173

Register of psychotherapists, including psychoanalysts, analytical psychologists, psychoanalytical psychotherapists and child psychotherapists.

British Psychological Society
St Andrew's House, 48 Princess Road East, Leicester LE1 7DR

0116 2549 568

Produces a directory of chartered clinical psycologists. The directory is also available in most reference libraries.

British Association for Behavioural and Cognitive Psychotherapy
c/o Harrow Psychological Health Services, Northwick Park Hospital, Watford Road, Harrow, Middlesex HA1 3UJ

Produces a directory of accredited cognitive behavioural practitioners. List is free but please encloses an SAE.

Institute for Counselling and Personal Development Trust
Interpoint, 20–24 York Street, Belfast BT15 1AQ

02890 330996

Offers counselling and psychotherapy (normally free), course for helpers and community training and development courses.

Debt (see also 'Welfare' below)

National Debtline
0645 500511

Dementia

Alzheimer's Disease Society (local groups)
Gordon House, 10 Greencoat Place, London SW1P 1PH

020 7306 0606

National Helpline: 0845 300336 8 am–6 pm
Support to families and friends of people with dementia.

Domestic violence

Women's Aid
National Helpline 0345 023468

Domestic Violence Unit or Community Safety Unit
Contact local Police Force for details

Depression

Depression Alliance (local groups)
35 Westminster Bridge Rd, London SE1 7JB

020 7633 9929 (Answerphone)

National network of self-help groups, information for people
suffering from depression and carers.

Aware Defeat Depression Ltd (local groups)
Depression Information Centre, 22 Great James Street,
Derry BT48 7DA

02871 260602

Provides information leaflets, lectures and runs support groups
for sufferers and relatives.

Association for Post-Natal Illness
25 Jerdan Place, London SW6 1BE

020 7386 0868 (Monday to Friday 10 am–5 pm)

Runs a network of volunteers to support sufferers throughout the UK. Leaflets available.

Seasonal Affective Disorders Association
PO Box 989, Steyning BN44 3HS

Information about Seasonal Affective Disorder (SAD). Offers advice and support to members.

Drug misuse

The Council for Involuntary Tranquilliser Addiction (CITA)
Cavendish House, Brighton Road, Waterloo, Liverpool L22 5NG

0151 474 9626
Helpline: 0151 949 0102 10 am–1 pm Monday to Friday

Support and information to help people withdraw from tranquillizers.

Narcotics Anonymous
For advice, information and counselling on drug addiction

020 7730 0009

For leaflets, telephone the UK Service Officer on 020 7251 4007.

Adfam National
Waterbridge House, 32–36 Loman Street, London SE1 0EE

Helpline: 020 7928 8900 10 am–5 pm Monday, Wednesday, Thursday and Friday, 10 am–6.45 pm Tuesday

Confidential support and information for families and friends of drug users.

Families Anonymous (local groups)
UK Office, Unit 37, The Doddington and Rollo Community Association, Charlotte Despard Avenue, Battersea, London SW11 5JE

020 7498 4680 Monday to Friday 1 pm–5 pm

Runs self-help groups in the UK for families and friends of those with a drug problem.

Release

Advice line: 020 7729 9904 10 am–6 pm

24-hr helpline: 020 7603 8654
Drugs in Schools helpline: 0345 366 666 10 am–5 pm
Monday–Friday

Advice, support and information to drug users, their families and
friends, on all aspects of drug use and drug-related legal
problems

Eating disorders

Centre for Eating Disorders (Scotland)
3 Sciennes Rd, Edinburgh EH9 1LE

0131 668 3051

Information, private psychotherapy, self-help manuals.

Eating Disorders Association
1st Floor, Wensum House, 103 Prince of Wales Road, Norwich
NR1 1DW

01603 619090
Helpline: 01603 621414 Monday to Friday 9 am–6.30 pm
Youth helpline (for under 19s): 01603 765050 4–6 pm weekdays

Information packs for patients and professionals, including pack
for puchasers.

Overeaters Anonymous (local groups)
01454 857158 (recorded message)

Self-help groups for those suffering form eating disorders or
overeating.

Anorexia Bulimia Careline
84 University Street, Belfast BT7 1HE

02890 614440.

Ethnic minorities

Commission for Racial Equality (local groups)
10 Allington Street, London SW1E 5EH

020 7828 7022

This is a statutory body set up under the Race Relations Act. It can help individuals with cases of racial discrimination and investigate instances of discrimination. It is a network of 80 or more Race Equality Councils in most of the UK's large towns and cities.

Jewish Association for the Mentally Ill (JAMI)
707 High Road, Finchley, London N12 0BT

020 8343 1111

Offers guidance, counselling and support to sufferers and carers. Runs a help and referral line.

NAFSIYAT
278 Seven Sisters Road, London N4 2HY

020 7263 4130

An intercultural therapy centre. Its own services are local; however, it may be able to assist in providing information about counsellors from black and ethnic minority groups in other areas of the UK.

Refugee Council
3 Bondway, London SW8 1SJ

020 7820 3000

Gives practical support and advice to refugees. Provides information on mental health services to refugees and their advisers.

Learning disability

Mencap
123 Golden Lane, London EC1Y 0RT

020 7454 0454
Information line: 020 7696 5593

Information and support for people with a learning disability and their families in the UK. Provides residential, employment, futher education and leisure and holiday services.

Mencap Northern Ireland
Segal House, 4 Annadale Avenue, Belfast BT7 3JH

02890 691351

Family Advisory Service Line: 0345 636227

Down's Syndrome Association
155 Mitcham Road, London SW17 9PG

020 8682 4001 (Tuesday, Wednesday and Thursday, 10 am–4 pm)

Information and support for people with Downs Syndrome and their families.

Scope (formerly the Spastic Society) — local groups
12 Park Crescent, London W1N 4EQ. Tel: 020 7636 5020

Website: http://www.scope.org.uk/

Freephone Cerebral Palsy Helpline: 0800 626216

Information, emotional support, and support groups for people with cerebral palsy and their families. Only some people with cerebral palsy have learning disabilities in addition to their physical disabilities.

National Autistic Society (local groups)
393 City Road, London EC1V 1NG

Helpline: 020 7903 3555
Office: 020 7833 2299

Information service, literature, national diagnostic and assessment service, supported employment scheme, befrienders and other services.

Mental health and illness — general

MIND (local groups)
Granta House, 15–19 Broadway, Stratford, London E15 4BQ

0208 519 2122

Variety of information sheets and booklets for users, local groups and other publications.

MINDinfoLINE

08457 660 163 (outside London)
020 8522 1728 (Greater London)

National telephone information service on Mental Health Issues.
Open 9.15 am–4.45 pm, Monday to Friday

SANELine

Helpline: 0345 678000 seven nights 2 pm–midnight

National helpline for mental health information.

Mental Health Drugs Helpline

Run by the UK Psychiatric Pharmacy Group and staffed by
experienced mental-health pharmacists, this provides
independent advice and information about drugs to patients and
carers.

020 7919 2999 (11 am–5 pm Monday–Friday, excluding Bank
Holidays).

Drug information website for service users

Run by the Chair of the Psychiatric Pharmacy Group, this site
contains detailed, user friendly information on psychiatric drugs.

URL: http://www.nmhc.co.uk.

Mental Health Foundation

20/21 Cornwall Terrace, London NW1 4QL

020 7535 7400

Has a series of free leaflets about mental illness and learning
disabilities for the general public.

Hearing Voices Network (local groups)

Dale House, 35 Dale Street, Manchester M1 2HF

0161 228 3896 Monday, Tuesday, Wednesday, Friday 10 am–3 pm;
answerphone at all other times

Self-help groups to allow people to explore their voice-hearing
experiences in a secure and confidential way. Information pack
available.

Cause for Mental Health
2 Castle Village, Carrickfer, County Antrim BT38 7BH

01960 367728
Helpline: 0845 6030291

Northern Ireland Association for Mental Health
Central Office, 80 University Street, Belfast BT7 1HE

02890 328474

Provides services in the community for people with mental-health needs and campaigns to increase public awareness of mental health issues.

Scottish Association for Mental Health
Cumbrae House, 15 Carlton Court, Glasgow G59JP

0141 568 7000

Information about any aspect of mental health.

Parents and children

Home-Start UK (local branches)
2 Salisbury Road, Leicester LE1 7QR

0116 233 9955. 8.30 am–5.15 pm

Volunteers offer support, friendship and practical support to young families with at least one child under five, who are experiencing difficulties and stress.

Parentline (and the National Stepfamily Association)
Helpline: 0808 8002222 (9 am–9 pm Monday to Friday, 9.30 am–5 pm Saturday, 10 am–3 pm Sunday)
Office: 01702 554782

Information sheets and books about belonging to a stepfamily: 020 7209 2460

Offers help and advice to parents on all aspects of bringing up children and teenagers. Provides support for parents under stress.

Parents Anonymous (local groups)
020 7263 8918

Offers friendship and help to parents who are at risk of abusing their children and those who may have done so. Offers telephone counselling and network of local groups.

Parent Network (local groups)
020 7735 1214

Self-help groups for parents.

Newpin (Northern Ireland) (local groups)
Development Office, 8 Windsor Avenue, Lurgan, County Armagh BT67 9BG

01762 324843

Befriending and support groups for parents of young children who are under stress. Work focuses on alleviating maternal depression and distress. Provides training in parenting skills, family play programmes.

Relationship problems

Relate (local groups)
Herbert Gray College, Little Church Street, Rugby CV21 3AP

01788 573241

Web site: www.relate.org.uk

For access to a network of local counselling and advice centres. Relationship counselling for couples or individuals over 16. Sex therapy for couples. Clients pay on a sliding scale.

Rapport — couple counselling
(Care for the Family) covers whole of UK

029 2081 1733.

Self-care for professionals

British Medical Association Stress Counselling Service
0645 200169

24-hr, free, confidential counselling service available to doctors, their families and medical students, to discuss personal, emotional and work related problems.

National Counselling Service for Sick Doctors
0170 935 5982

Confidential advisory service. Deals with concerns about own health or that of a colleague.

Medical Council on Alcoholism
020 7487 4445

Royal College of Nursing

0345 726 100

24-hr service for information and advice. Calls charged at local rates. Service is free.

Schizophrenia

National Schizophrenia Fellowship (local groups)
28 Castle Street, Kingston-upon-Thames, Surrey KT1 1SS

020 8547 3937

NSF (Scotland), Claremont House, 130 East Claremont St, Edinburgh EI IT 4LB

0131 557 8969

NSF (Northern Ireland), 'Wyndhurst', Knockbracken Health Care Park, Saintfield Rd, Belfast BT8 8BH

01232 402 323

Monthly social groups for clients with schizophrenia living in the community and relatives support.

Self-harm

Bristol Crisis Service for Women
PO Box 654, Bristol BS99 1SH

0117 925 1119 (office and helpline)

Helpline: Friday and Saturday night 9 pm–12.30 am

Telephone counselling and information service relating to self-injury. Bi-monthly newsletter *Shout* on self-harm.

Basement Project
PO Box 5, Abergavenny, Gwent NP7 5XW

01873 856 524

Publications on self-harm, run groups and workshops and work with people (mainly women) who have been abused. They have a national forum of people who work with self-harm.

National Self-Harm Network
PO Box 16150, London NW1 3WW

They provide information sheets and training, and campaign for the understanding of people who self-harm.

Suicidal feelings

Samaritans (local groups)
National Office — administration only: 10 The Grove, Slough, Berks SL1 1QP

01753 532713

Support by listening for those feeling lonely, despairing or suicidal.

UK-wide telephone helpline: 0345 909090
Website: www.samaritans.org.uk

CALM (for young men)
Helpline: 0800 58 58 58

Trauma

Trauma Aftercare Trust (TACT)
Buttfields, The Farthings, Withington, Glos GL54 4DF

01242 890498 (Administration)
24-hr helpline: 01242 890306

Provides information about counselling and treatment for post-traumatic stress disorder

Victim Support
National Office, Cranmer House, 39 Brixton Road, London SW9 6DZ

020 7735 9166; Fax: 020 7582 5712

Victim Supportline
PO Box 11431, London SW9 6ZH

0845 30 30 900 (9 am–9 pm, Monday–Friday; 9 am–7 pm, Saturday and Sunday; 9 am–5 pm, Bank Holidays)

Provides emotional support and practical information for anyone has suffered the effects of crime, regardless of whether the crime has been reported.

Welfare and advice for practical problems

Citizens Advice Bureau (See local telephone directory for nearest one)
National Association of Citizens Advice Bureau: 020 7833 2181

Provide a wide range of free and confidential advice and help. Subjects inlcude social security benefits, housing, family and personal mattters, money advice and consumer complaints.

Benefits Enquiry Line
0800 882200

For information about Disability Living Allowance and Invalid Care Allowance and other benefits.

Shelter Helpline
0800 446441

Free 24-hr helpline, giving general advice and help on housing problems.

Mental health in your practice: what does your practice offer?

You may like to consider the following:

Practice organization:

1. A practice policy for what receptionists should do when faced with a patient who is very agitated or anxious.
2. Some longer slots booked in surgeries to allow for people with emotional problems.
3. Routine follow-up appointments for people prescribed antidepressants, with a doctor or another member of the team.
4. Encouraging patients with chronic mental disorders to see the same team member at each visit.
5. A register of patients with severe or chronic mental illness to ensure regular follow-up and monitoring.
6. Reviewing the 'mental health workload' of each partner. If it falls disproportionately on one or a small number of partners, consider ways of relieving the pressure; alternatively, consider acknowledging and supporting the partners' specialization as part of the way the team operates.

Information and support for patients:

7. Information leaflets or audio-tapes for people suffering mental ill health.
8. Information readily available to patients and all members of the practice team about community or voluntary groups who can help patients suffering mental ill health.

Skills within the primary-care team:

9. Reviewing the skills of all members of the team — doctors, health visitor, practice nurse, counsellor, district nurse, school nurse. What kinds of problems/patients is each competent to deal with? Are all members of the team aware of the skills already available within the team?
10. Checking the training and support needs of practice nurses or others who are involved in activities, such as giving depot injections or monitoring of lithium.
11. Developing further primary mental-health skills within the team. Consider:

- structured problem-solving
- activity planning — depression
- teaching controlled breathing — anxiety
- teaching relaxation — anxiety
- motivational interviewing — alcohol and drug misuse
- supporting graded exposure to feared situations — anxiety, particularly phobias
- encouraging more appropriate thinking (cognitive skills) — depression and anxiety
- re-attribution of symptoms from physical to emotional causes
- asking about suicidal intentions
- managing self-harming behaviours.

12. Seriously considering clinical supervision, peer or external, for team members who take on a significant counselling or mental health work load.

Liaison with community mental-health and substance-abuse services:

13. Regular, face-to-face meetings with the relevant person from the community mental health team(s) which serve your practice.
14. Arrangements to 'share' people with a severe mental illness and those with substance abuse.
15. Displaying the contact details of the key worker for each person with a severe mental illness prominently on the patient notes.

Psychological therapies:

16. Reviewing the access, via secondary care or non-statutory agencies, to cognitive, behavioural, family or other psychological therapies.

Stress management for the primary-care team:

17. Meeting with members of the practice team to consider how you might provide support for each other to minimize your own stress.
18. Liaison with the primary care group to consider some form of regular psychological support system for health professionals.

Further reading and websites

Clinical

Andrews G, Jenkins R (eds). *Management of Mental Disorders* (UK edition). Sydney: World Health Organization Collaborating Centre for Mental Health and Substance Abuse, 1999.
Excellent, accessible textbook for use by GPs and generalist mental-health clinicians working in community settings. Lots of practical advice, resource materials and assessment instruments. Covers core management skills, medication, affective disorders, anxiety and somatoform disorders, schizophrenic disorders, dieting disorders, substance-use disorders, child and adolescent disorders, personality problems, sexual dysfunction and sleep disorders.

Armstrong E. *Mental Health Issues in Primary Care: a Practical Guide*. Basingstoke: Macmillan Press, 1995.
Written for generalist nurses in primary care by a health visitor and mental-health educator. Discusses treatments available and strategies for prevention for depression, anxiety and schizophrenia

Taylor D, McConnel D, Abel K, Kerwin R. *The Bethlem and Maudsley NHS Trust Prescribing Guidelines*. London: Martin Dunnitz Ltd, 1999.
Provides detailed, annually updated information on prescribing psychotropic drugs. Helpful charts and flow charts.

Bazire S. *GP's Psychotropic Handbook (2nd edition)*. Salisbury: Quay Books, 1998
Compact, up-to-date information on psychiatric drugs. Contains community oriented information.

Padesky C, Greenberger D. *Clinicians Guide to Mind over Mood*. New York: Guilford Press, 1995.
Guide to cognitive therapy. Supports clinicians in acting as guides to patients using the companion volume *Mind over Mood: a Cognitive Treatment Manual for Clients*. Suitable for use by primary-care counsellors, or others with appropriate training.

Daines B, Gask L, Usherwood T. *Medical and Psychiatric Issues for Counsellors*. London: Sage, 1997.

Proudfood J. *Beating the Blues*. London: Ultramind Group plc, 1999.
Eight-session, interactive, multimedia therapy programme for the treatment of anxiety and depression. Department of Psychology, Institute of Psychiatry Maudsley Hospital, De Crespigny Park, Denmark Hill, London SE5 8AF. Phone: 020 7600 6777.

Service development in primary care

Mental Health Foundation. *Knowing Our Own Minds: a Survey of How People in Emotional Distress Take Control of Their Lives*, 1997.
Valuable summary of what people with mental-health problems find useful; many simple, cost effective options.

Byng R, Single H. *Developing Primary Care for Patients with Long-term Mental Illness: Your Guide to Improving Services*. London: Kings Fund, 1999.
Practical guide for primary-care teams and community mental-health teams to developing shared care.

Clinical Standards Advisory Group. *Services for Patients With Depression*. London: Department of Health, 1999.
Evidence-based standards for services for depression, review of state of current services and recommendations for improving services. Focuses largely on primary care.

Gask L, Sibbald B, Creed F. Evaluating models of working at the interface between mental health services and primary care. Br J Psychiatry 1997, 170: 6–11.

Guide to setting up and running a managed primary care counselling service. Counselling in Primary Care. 95 Hewarts Lane, Bognor Regis, West Sussex PO21 3DJ. Tel: 01243 268 322.

Cohen A, Paton J. *Developing an Integrated Mental Health Service: a Workbook for Primary Care Groups*. London: Sainsbury Centre for Mental Health, 1999.

Internet resources for mental health

Centre for Evidence-Based Mental Health
This centre has established a website with extracts from the journal *Evidence-Based Mental Health*, which includes a useful evidence-based mental health toolkit. It is a gateway to many other related sites through its links.
URL: http://www.cebmh.com/

The Cochrane Collaboration
URL: http://www.update-software.com/ccweb/default.htm

NHS Centre for Reviews and Dissemination
URL: http://www.york.ac.uk/inst/crd/welcome.htm

Health Evidence Bulletins Wales
URL: http://www.uwcm.ac.uk/uwcm/lb/pep

Institute of Psychiatry, Kings College, London
URL: http://www.iop.kcl.ac.uk/main
See the Institute's library page for links to other resources.

Mental Health Foundation
URL: http://www.mentalhealth.org.uk

PriMHE (Primary Care Mental Health Education)
Information and links specific to primary care mental health.
URL: http://www.primhe.org

UK Psychiatric Pharmacy Group
Useful resources section, including 'Bespoke', an individualized patient information system.
URL: http://www.ukppg.co.uk

What do the different mental-health professionals do?

Community mental-health teams
Community mental-health teams provide assessment, treatment and care for individuals and groups, outside hospitals. They comprise a mix of the professionals described below but not all are represented in every team. Community psychiatric nurses (CPNs) are the most numerous.

Psychiatrists
These are doctors who have specialized in mental health and who work both in hospitals and, increasingly, in the community. They are responsible for diagnosis, the general mental health and physical care of patients, including medication, and have specific responsibilities in the implementation of the Mental Health Act. Some have further specialist training in areas such as the psychiatry of old age or psychotherapy.

Psychiatric nurses
These are the most numerous professionals in mental health. Most of their basic training takes place in hospital.

Community psychiatric nurses
CPNs are usually registered mental nurses, some of whom have completed the ENB training for community work. They are based in the community and care for people with mental illness in their own homes and communities. Their role can include psychological therapies, long-term support, counselling and administering medication by 'depot' injection.

Clinical psychologists
Clinical psychologists have a degree in psychology and a postgraduate qualification in clinical work. They play a key role in assessment and may carry out a wide range of treatments, such as behavioural therapy and cognitive therapy. They may provide training and supervision in this kind of work to other professionals.

Psychotherapists, psychoanalysts and counsellors

These professionals all offer 'talking treatments'. The methods, intensity of treatment and the length of time involved varies. Individual or group therapy may be offered. Many psychotherapists are also psychiatrists, psychologists or nurses. Primary-care counsellors offer a brief, focused intervention across a wide spectrum of mild to moderate disorders.

Occupational therapists

OTs work in hospital and in the community. Their role is to help people to develop confidence and skills in daily living, using a variety of techniques, such as creative therapies and training in practical tasks.

Mental-health social workers

Mental-health social workers have a general qualification in social work and may have specialized later in mental health. They act as care managers:

- assessing people with severe and complex needs
- working closely with health colleagues
- coordinating and monitoring care plans
- ensuring service users get the services they need — respite care, residential accommodation, supported housing, or support from a community care worker.

Less frequently, they may also provide formal counselling or psychotherapy.

Approved social workers (ASW) — in Scotland: Mental health officers

These have undertaken specialist training in mental health and are approved under the Mental Health Act 1983 (in Scotland, the Mental Health Act 1984, and in Northern Ireland, the Mental Health Order 1986), to carry out the following duties:

- Assessments for urgent admission to hospital — approved social work assessments under the Mental Health Act
- Acting as supervisors under the supervised discharge procedures
- Acting as social supervisors for mentally disordered offenders subject to Home Office supervision.

Community care workers/support workers

Community care workers are non-professional members of the community mental-health team, who support and encourage people to regain or maintain their confidence and independence by offering help in the following ways:

Practical:
- Budgeting/debt management
- Employment-paid and unpaid
- Social contact/using community resources
- Daily living skills
- Advocacy/negotiation with other agencies
- Life and social skills.

Emotional:
- Listening
- Confidence-building
- Esteem-building
- Stress/anxiety management
- Continuous regular contact.

Day care services

Day care services aim to provide a number of groups that offer a supportive environment, and a safe space to relax in. This helps people build self-esteem and confidence, while giving an opportunity to meet others. Drop-in sessions, sports and activity groups, and outings are all included as part of the day service.

Child guidance and child psychiatric clinics

These are usually staffed by a multidisciplinary team, including psychologists, social workers, specialist nurses and play therapists. Child psychiatric assessments usually involve the child and his/her parents. Sometimes, the whole family is involved. With the family's permission, contact with the school is often made.

Educational psychologists and education welfare officers

Provide a service for schools and help with problems associated with school.

Learning disability teams

Learning disability teams (similar to community mental-health teams) provide specialist health and social care services. Multidisciplinary teams usually include community learning disability nurses, psychiatrists, psychologists, speech and language therapists, physiotherapists, occupational therapists and may also include a dietitian.

Psychological therapies: what are they?

Behavioural therapy

Behaviour therapy is based on the belief that many of our actions are the result of things that we have learned. The focus of behavioural interventions is on definable behaviours which can be readily monitored and addressed in therapeutic interventions. It is a very directive therapy which sets objectives (in collaboration with the patient) for the patient to attain. Patients are given homework assignments. It is particularly good for treating phobias, obsessional and compulsive behaviour and can also be helpful in dealing with some sexual problems. Anxiety management and exposure therapy are particular types of behavioural therapies.

Anxiety management

This approach involves a varying mixture of behavioural strategies often taught in a group setting to people with anxiety problems. The strategies commonly include education about the nature of anxiety (eg fight-or-flight-response), recognising hyperventilation, the slow breathing technique, relaxation training and graded exposure. Stress management, assertiveness training and structured problem-solving may also be included, depending upon the training and background of the therapist and the needs of the clients.

Graded exposure

Patients who avoid particular places or people because of anxiety (ie those suffering from phobias, obsessive compulsive disorder or panic) are encouraged to gradually face the things that they fear, starting with easy situations and building up slowly to harder things. Breathing and relaxation techniques are used to help the patient remain in the feared situation until the anxiety diminishes and the patient learns that they can cope with the situation. The clinician supports the clients but does not need to accompany them in their assignments.

Cognitive therapy

Cognitive therapy is based on the idea that how you think largely determines the way you feel. Cognitive therapy teaches the

143

individual to recognise and challenge upsetting thoughts.
Learning to challenge negative or fear-inducing thoughts helps
people think more realistically and feel better. Patients are given
homework assignments. Cognitive therapy is more complex than
positive thinking. It is usually given in fifty minute sessions over
10–15 weeks.

Cognitive behavioural therapy (CBT)

This is a structured treatment combining elements of cognitive
and behavioural therapy approaches, used to change a patient's
thought processes and behaviour in order to bring about relief of
symptoms or other practical objectives agreed by the patient. The
range of techniques used includes challenging irrational beliefs,
replacing the irrational beliefs with alternative ones, thought
stopping, exposure, assertiveness and social skills training.
Patients are given homework assignments.

Compliance therapy

This is a form of counselling, usually used for people with severe
mental illness who are reluctant to take medication. It encourages
patients to take an active role in monitoring their illness and
negotiating treatment decisions. The patient's views about
medication are elicited, ambivalence explored and options
considered in an atmosphere of support and empathy, avoiding
blaming. This interactive approach has proved more successful
than a simple didactic approach.

Counselling

The term 'counselling' covers a wide range of skills and
techniques. Counsellors may, for example, use cognitive or
behavioural techniques. In the main, however, it provides a
supportive and non-judgemental atmosphere for people to talk
over their problems and explore more satisfactory ways of living.
Counselling generally deals with specific life situations and is
more short term than analytical psychotherapies — in primary
care, usually 6–12 sessions. It is generally used for less severe
problems. Counselling is often focused, with counsellors or
agencies specializing in particular problems, eg relationship
problems, rape or bereavement.

Family interventions for people with schizophrenia

A form of 'psycho-social intervention', this comprises giving
information to the patient's family about the illness, and helping
them to improve their ability and confidence in tackling problems

effectively. The approach is broadly behavioural and the family is encouraged to set realistic goals. This means that the family is able to avoid making unrealistic demands of the patient, making the environment of the person who is ill less stressful. Relapse rates are reduced.

Interpersonal therapy

Interpersonal psychotherapy uses the connection between the onset of symptoms and current interpersonal problems as a treatment focus. It deals with current, rather than past, relationships, and maintains a clear focus on the patient's social context and dysfunction rather than their personality. Treatment is carried out by experienced therapists over 10–15 sessions.

Problem-solving

Structured problem-solving can help patients sort out and deal with stresses that contribute to worry and depression. It involves encouraging the patient to identify specific problems, to order them in terms of importance and then to focus on one problem at a time, writing down potential solutions and identifying specific steps that he/she might take to implement the solutions. A main aim is to assist people to incorporate the principles of efficient problem-solving and goal achievement into their everyday lives. The aim is not for the clinician to solve everyone's problems for them but to give people skills so that they can effectively overcome problems and achieve goals for themselves. Self-management is a key goal, with the clinician adopting the role of teacher or guide.

Psychodynamic therapy (analytical psychotherapies)

These are usually offered by psychotherapy departments after assessment by a psychotherapist. They are based on psychoanalytical ways of understanding human development (Freud and his successors). The therapy concentrates on unconscious conflicts and explores the person's inner world, as well as his or her external situations. Analytical therapies may be offered on an individual, couple, family or group basis. Individual sessions are usually for 50 min over several months. Group sessions usually last an hour a week for a year or more. Couple and family sessions are usually more wide spread, with homework tasks set between sessions.

Training for primary-care teams in mental-health skills

This is a template for a chart for information on local and regional sources of training and support. You might like to compare this with the review of the training needs of your practice team or primary care organization/local health group. On the next page, we have listed some national resources which may be drawn upon to help fill identified local gaps. The list of national resources is not exhaustive.

Topic	Multi-disciplinary training	GPs	Nurses	Receptionists/non-professionals	Counsellors
Mental-health awareness					
Communication skills					
Counselling skills					
Problem-solving					
Cognitive strategies					
Motivational interviewing					
Depression					
Post-natal depression					
Anxiety					
Schizophrenia					
Dementia					
Re-attribution — somatization					
Suicide and self-harm					
Child and adolescent mental health					
Alcohol misuse					
Drug misuse					

The following providers of courses or training packs are all national organizations. You may wish to adapt this list to include details of your local or regional providers of training.

Training courses

Training courses may be organized locally via Educational Consortia, university departments of General Practice or Nursing, Health Authorities or primary care groups, often utilizing locally available skills. The following provide courses or training packs on a national or regional basis.

Royal College of General Practitioners Unit for Mental Health Education in Primary Care regularly runs courses for people wishing to teach mental-health skills to primary-care teams in their local areas. The emphasis is on provision of flexible, inpractice, multidisciplinary training to teams. Those attending usually operate as pairs (eg GP–nurse, or GP–counsellor) in their work with practices. This 'National Teachers Course on Mental Health Management in Primary Care' can be provided in different parts of the country, depending upon demand. The course is modular, with practical experience between modules. There is also an ongoing network of people who have attended the course and are working as educators in primary care. Contact Dr Andre Tylee, Director of RCGP Unit for Mental Health Education in Primary Care, Institute of Psychiatry, De Crespigny Park, Denmark Hill, London SE5 8AF. Tel: 020 7919 3150

The Depression Care Training Centre provides a range of courses including:

- accredited two-day course for all general nurses in primary care settings ('Caring for people with depression');
- multi-professional, module-based programme for primary care teams ('Recognition and management of depression' — a series of half day sessions);
- Trainers' course: Three-day course to train and license up to 10 people to lead depression care training courses in their own area. Carries a compulsory assessment;
- One-day course for general nurses on Schizophrenia.

Training can be provided nationwide. Contact Elizabeth Armstrong or Martin Davies, National Depression Care Training Centre, Nene University, Thornby 1, Park Campus, Boughton Green Road, Northampton NN2 7AL. Tel: 01604 735500 ext 2640/2712. Email: liz.armstrong@nene.ac.uk.

PriMHE (Primary care Mental Health Education) is an initiative to bring together health professionals active in primary mental-health care to provide a nationally coordinated programme of mental health education. Discussion forums for teachers, researchers and primary care group/LHG mental health leads. Co-chairs are Professor André Tylee and Dr Chris Manning. For information about their journal, network, educational meetings, training materials and training programme, contact PriMHE Secretariat, 29 Park Road, Hampton Wick, Surrey KT1 4AS. Tel: 020 8977 7173. Email: info@primhe.org. Website: URL http://www.Primhe.org.

The National Primary Care Research and Development Centre runs a modular course for GP Registrars in 'Managing mental disorders in primary care' and other courses on a needs basis. Contact Dr Linda Gask, Reader in Psychiatry, University of Manchester, Department of Community Psychiatry, Royal Preston Hospital, Sharoe Green Lane, Preston PR2 9HT. Tel: 01772 710 071/2.

The National Primary Care Facilitation Programme runs a course on 'Facilitation in Primary Care'. It also runs an educational and support network for primary care facilitators who include mental health in their work. Contact the Mental Health Development Officer, The National Primary Care Facilitation Programme, Block 10, The Churchill, The Oxford Radcliffe Hospital, Oxford OX3 7LJ. Tel: 01865 226 076/35.

The Counselling in Primary Care Trust keeps information about additional training for counsellors in issues particular to work in general practice, including a postgraduate diploma course. Contact Dr Graham Curtis-Jenkins, Counselling in Primary Care Trust, Majestic House, High Street, Staines TW18 4DG. Tel: 01784 441 782.

Resources for use by trainers

Training packages, including videos, for use in skills-based training (watching the skills demonstrated on the video followed by practising them in role play) are available on the following topics:

- Managing somatic presentation of emotional distress (re-attribution, 2nd edition)
- Helping people at risk of suicide or self-harm
- Problem-based interviewing in general practice.

Contact Nick Jordan, Video Producer, University of Manchester, Dept of Psychiatry, Withington Hospital, West Didsbury, Manchester M20 2LR. Tel: 0161 291 4359. Email: Nick.Jordan@man.ac.uk. Online catalogue: www.man.ac.uk/psych.

Other topics available include:

- Anxiety (non-pharmacological approaches)
- Dementia
- Chronic fatigue
- Psychosis in general practice

from Dr Andre Tylee, RCGP Unit for Mental Health Education in Primary Care, Institute of Psychiatry, De Crespigny Park, Denmark Hill, London SE5 8AF. Tel: 020 7919 3150

- Counselling depression

from the Royal College of Psychiatrists, 17 Belgrave Square, London SW1X 8PG. Tel: 020 7235 2351

- Problem-solving

available from Dr L Mynors Wallace, Warneford Hospital, Oxford

- Alcohol misuse (including motivational interviewing)

from Dr Barry Lewiss, Department of Post-Graduate Medicine, Gateway House, Piccadilly South, Manchester M60 7LP. Tel: 0161 237 2109

- Child and adolescent mental health

available from Professor Elena Garralda, Academic Unit of Child and Adolescent Psychiatry, Saint Mary's Hospital, Praed Street, Paddington, London W2 1NY. Tel: 020 7886 1145.

Audio tapes on depression and anxiety for patients and for primary care professionals are available from Wendy Lloyd Audio Productions Ltd, 30 Guffitts Rake Meols, Wirral L47 7AD. Tel: 0151 632 0662.

An interactive compact disc teaching/revising basic clinical skills for primary care clinicians is produced by the Clinical Research Unit for Anxiety Disorders (CRUFAD) in Australia, which is a WHO Collaborating Centre for Mental Health and Substance Abuse. The CD-Rom covers interviewing skills, prescribing skills, patient education, structured problem-solving and control of hyperventilation. It costs A$70. Details of this and many other resources, usually based on cognitive behavioural methods, including treatment manuals (suitable for use by counsellors or others with appropriate training) on obsessional compulsive disorder, panic, generalized anxiety and phobias can be found on CRUFAD's website: http://www.crufad.unsw.edu.au, or by contacting Professor Gavin Andrews, University of New South Wales Clinical Research Unit for Anxiety Disorders, 299 Forbes Street, Darlinghurst, NSW 2010, Australia. Fax: (612) 9332 4316. E-mail: gavina@gecko.crufad.unsw.edu.au.

A video, training manual and nurse interview schedule to help nurses and others in primary care learn how to detect depression in elderly people is available from Professor Anthony Mann, Institute of Psychiatry, De Crespigny Park, Denmark Hill, London SE5 8AF.

'The Primary Care of Mental Health — Team Training Programme' training pack for guided use by primary-care teams in their own surgery is available from Royal Institute of Health and Public Hygiene, 28 Portland Place, London W1N 4DE.

CALIPSO, at the University of Leeds, provide interactive CD-ROM self-led learning resources for use by GPs, trainee psychiatrists and others, in assessment and management of mood disorders, depression, anxiety, schizophrenia and paranoid disorders, and dementia. Also, they produce two CD-ROM self-help packages for patients on overcoming depression and overcoming bulimia. For prices and other details, contact the University of Leeds Innovations Ltd., 175 Woodhouse Lane, Leeds LS2 3AR. Tel: 0113 233 3444. E-mail: s.taylor-parker@ulis.co.uk. URL: www.calipso.co.uk

'RCN Nursing Update' produces the following Learning Units: Unit 27 — *Lifting the Cloud*; Unit 28 — *Suicide: a Target for Health*; Unit 049 — *Best Practice in Counselling Skills*; Unit 068 — *Depression — Moving On*. Details from Royal College of Nursing Institute, Nursing Update Office, 20 Cavendish Square, London W1M 0AB. Tel: 020 7409 3333.

A learning resource pack for use by health professionals and others on 'Understanding Depression in People with Learning Disabilities' is available from Pavilion Publishing Ltd., 8 St. George's Place, Brighton BN1 4ZZ. Tel: 01273 623222. Price: £125 plus VAT and p&p.

A variety of other resources for trainers are available from MIND, the Mental Health Foundation and the Samaritans. For example, the Mental Health Foundation sells a training pack, *Working With People Who Self Injure*, and MIND provides inhouse training on mental health awareness and other mental health issues. These training resources are generally aimed at a broad audience, including clinicians, but are not specifically produced for primary care. For catalogues, contact MIND Conference and Training Unit, Granta House, 15–19 Broadway, London E15 4BQ, and The Mental Health Foundation, 20/21 Cornwall Terrace, London NW1 4QL.

Support network for primary-care groups and local health groups

The Royal College of Psychiatrists is working with partners from primary care to plan support to primary care organizations and LHGs regarding clinical governance for mental health. Contact Tim Kendall, Royal College of Psychiatrists Research Unit, 11Grosvenor Crescent, London SW1X 7EE. Tel: 020 7235 2351. E-mail: timkendallCRULondon@compuserve.com.

References

References are graded A–C, I–V, as discussed in the introduction and in the key on p. 5.

1 Birchwood M. Early intervention in schizophrenia: theoretical background and clinical strategies. *Br J Clin Psychol* 1992, 31: 257–278. (BIV)

For more information about early detection of psychosis, see the Early Psychosis Prevention and Intervention Centre (EPPIC). *The Early Psychosis Training Pack.* Cheshire, UK: Gardiner-Caldwell Communications Ltd, 1997. Tel: (03) 9342 2800. URL: www.eppic.org.au

2 World Health Organization. Schizophrenia: an international follow-up study. Chichester: John Wiley & Sons, 1979. (AIV)

Large outcome study with two-year follow-up, showed that only 10–15% of patients did not recover from their illness in that two year period. Another, shorter term follow-up study show 83% of first episode psychotic patients treated with anti-psychotic medication remitting by one year post -inpatient admission. (Lieberman J, Jody D, Geisler S *et al.* Time course and biologic correlates of treatment response in first episode schizophrenia. *Arch Gen Psychiatry* 1993, 50: 369–376.)

3 Kavanagh DJ. Recent developments in expressed emotion and schizophrenia. *Br J Psychiatry* 1992, 160: 601–620. (AIII)

Family support and education, which promotes a more supportive family environment, can reduce relapse rates substantially.

4 Driver and Vehicle Licensing Agency. *At a Glance Guide to Medical Aspects of Fitness to Drive.* Swansea: DVLA, 1998.

Further information is available from The Senior Medical Adviser, DVLA, Driver Medical Unit, Longview Road, Morriston, Swansea SA99 ITU, Wales.

5a Mental Health Commission. *Early Intervention in Psychosis: Guidance Note.* Wellington, New Zealand, 1999.

b Falloon I, Coverdale J, Laidlaw T *et al.* Family management in the prevention of morbidity of schizophrenia: social outcome of a two-year longitudinal study. *Psychol Med* 1998, 17: 59–66.

Involvement of the family is vital. Education is important for engaging individuals and families in treatment and promoting recovery. Psychological therapies may be helpful.

6 Atypical antipsychotics appear to be better tolerated, with fewer extrapyramidal side-effects, than typical drugs at therapeutic doses. Even at low doses, extrapyramidal side-effects are commonly experienced with typical drugs. Whether or not atypicals improve the long-term outcome has yet to be established. Risperidone, amisulpride and possibly olanzapine have a dose-related effect. Selected references (BII):

a American Psychiatric Association. Practice guidelines: schizophrenia. *Am J Psychiatry* 1997, 154(Suppl 4): 1–49.

This reports 60% of patients, receiving acute treatment with typical antipsychotic medication, develop significant extrapyramidal side-effects.

b   Zimbroff D, Kane J, Tamminga CA *et al.* Controlled, dose-response study of sertindole and haloperidol in the treatment of schizophrenia. *Am J Psychiatry* 1997, 154: 782–791.

Haloperidol produced extrapyramidal symptoms at 4 mg/day.

c   Mir S, Taylor D. Issues in schizophrenia. *Pharmaceut J* 1998, 261: 55–58.

This paper reviews evidence on efficacy, safety and patient tolerability of atypical antipsychotics.

d   Duggan L, Fenton M, Dardennes RM, El-Dosoky A, Indran S. Olanzapine for schizophrenia. Cochrane Library, Oxford: Update Software, 1999.

e   Kennedy E, Song F, Hunter R, Gilbody S. Risperidone versus conventional antipsychotic medication for schizophrenia. Cochrane Library, Issue 2, 1998.

7   People suffering first episode of psychosis develop side-effects at lower doses of antipsychotic drugs than patients who are used to these drugs. For patients treated with high potency typical antipsychotics who are used to the drugs, the mean dose at which extrapyramidal side-effects appear is below the average clinically effective dose. The average clinically effective dose for those suffering a first episode has not yet been established, but clinical practice indicates that it is significantly lower than for patients used to the drugs. Selected references (BIII):

a   McEvoy JP, Hogarty GE, Steingard S. Optimal dose of neuroleptic in acute schizophrenia: a controlled study of the neuroleptic threshold and higher haloperidol dose. *Arch Gen Psychiatry* 1991, 48: 739–745.

First episode patients developed extrapyramidal side-effects at mean doses of haloperidol of 2.1 mg/day ±1.1 mg/day, whereas 'experienced' patients did so at mean dose of 4.3 ±2.4 mg/day.

b   See reference 6a.

Optimal therapeutic dose for most patients appears to be in the range of 6–12 mg/day haloperidol or equivalent. Evidence on optimal dose for first-onset patients is not yet clear.

8   Bollini P, Pampallona S, Orza MJ *et al.* Antipsychotic drugs: is more worse? A meta-analysis of the published randomized control trials. *Psychol Med* 1994, 24: 307–316. (AI)

For most patients, higher than moderate doses bring increased side-effects but no additional therapeutic gains.

9   A1 Dixon LB, Lehman AF, Levine J. Conventional antipsychotic medications for schizophrenia. *Schizophrenia Bull* 1995, 21(4): 567–577.

This paper presents overwhelming evidence that continuing maintenance therapy reduces risk of relapse. Concludes that it is appropriate to taper or discontinue medication within six months to a year for first-episode patients who experience a full remission of symptoms.

10   Taylor D, McConnell D, Abel K, Kerwin R. *The Bethlem and Maudsley NHS Trust Prescribing Guidelines*. London: Martin Dunitz Ltd, 1999.

Available from Martin Dunitz, 7–9 Pratt St, London NW1 OAE, UK. Tel: 0207 482 2202. Price: £11.99 plus £2 postage and packaging.

11 Consensus (BV). As people reacting to stresses such as unemployment or divorce are at high risk of developing a mental disorder, however, studies on prevention in high-risk groups may be relevant. These support the offering of social support and problem solving. (NHS Centre for Reviews and Dissemination. Mental health promotion in high-risk groups. *Effect Health Care Bull* 1997, 3(3): 1–10.)

12 Catalan J, Gath D, Edmonds G, Ennis J. The effects of not prescribing anxiolytics in general practice. *Br J Psychiatry* 1984, 144: 593–602.

This work demonstrates that GP advice and reassurance is as effective as administration of benzodiazepines. Mean time spent by the GP for giving advice and reassurance was 12 minutes, compared with 10.5 minutes for giving prescription.

13a Roth AD, Fonagy P. *What Works For Whom? A Critical Review of Psychotherapy Research*. New York: Guilford Press, 1996. (CII)

This book concludes that the efficacy of counselling in primary care settings is difficult to assess because of the methodological problems of available research. It seems more appropriate for milder presentations of disorders, however, than for more severe presentations, and that evidence is better for counselling focused on a particular client group (eg relationship or bereavement counselling).

b A Cochrane review will soon be available: Rowland N, Mellor Clark J, Bower P *et al*. *The Effectiveness and Cost-Effectiveness of Counselling in Primary Care*. Cochrane Database of Systematic Reviews.

14 Rosenberg H. Prediction of controlled drinking by alcoholics and problem drinkers. *Psychol Bull* 1993, 113: 129–139. (BII)

This is a qualitative review of the literature. Successful achievement of controlled drinking is associated with less severe dependence and a belief that controlled drinking is possible.

15 NHS Centre for Reviews and Dissemination. Brief interventions and alcohol use. *Effect Health Care Bull* 1993, 1: 1–12. (AI)

Brief interventions, including assessing drinking and related problems, motivational feedback and advice, are effective. They are most successful for less severely affected patients.

16 McCrady B, Irvine S. Self-help groups. In: Hester R, Miller W, Wilmsford N (eds). *Handbook of Alcoholism Treatment Approaches*. New York: Pergamon Press, 1989. (AIV)

This chapter discusses the characteristics of patients who are good candidates for Alcoholics Anonymous. Several studies show AA to be an important support in remaining alcohol-free to patients who are willing to attend.

17 American Psychiatric Association. *Practice Guidelines: Substance Use Disorders*, 1996. (BIV)

Where patients have mild to moderate withdrawal symptoms, general support, reassurance and frequent monitoring is sufficient treatment for two thirds of them, without pharmacological treatment.

18 Collins MN, Burns T, Van den Berk PA, Tubman GF. A structured programme for out-patient alcohol detoxification. *Br J Psychiatry* 1990, 156: 871–874. (BIV)

19 Duncan D, Taylor D. Chlormethiazole or chlordiazepoxide in alcohol detoxification. *Psychiatr Bull* 1996, 20: 599–601. (AIV)

This paper describes randomized controlled trials that show chlordiazepoxide and chlormethiazole to be of equal efficacy, and uncontrolled studies showing that chlormethiazole has generally mild adverse effects, while those of chlordiazepoxide may be very serious.

20 Tallaksen C, Bohmer T, Bell H. Blood and serum thiamin and thiamin phosphate esters concentrations in patients with alcohol dependence syndrome before and after thiamin treatment. *Alcohol Clin Exp Res* 1992, 16: 320–325. (BIV)

21 Kranzler H, Burleson J, Del Boca F *et al*. Buspirone treatment of anxious alcoholics: a placebo-controlled trial. *Arch Gen Psychiatry* 1994, 51: 720–731. (BII)

22 Department of Health, Scottish Office, Welsh Office, DHSS Northern Ireland. *Drug Misuse and Dependence — Guidelines on Clinical Management*, 1999.

23 Alcohol Concern. *Brief Interventions Guidelines*. London, 1997.

Available from Alcohol Concern, Waterbridge House, 32–36 Loman Street, London SE1 OEE, UK. Tel: 020 7928 7377.

24 Holder H, Longabaugh R, Miller W, Rubonis A. The cost effectiveness of treatment for alcoholism: a first approximation. *J Stud Alcohol* 1991, 52: 517–540. (AI)

Treatments aim to improve self-control and social skills, eg relationship skills, assertiveness and drink refusal.

25 Hunt G, Azrin N. A community reinforcement approach to alcoholism. *Behav Res Ther* 1973, 11: 91–104. (AI)

This approach uses behavioural principles and includes training in job-finding, support in developing alcohol-free social and recreational activities, and an alcohol-free social club.

26 Raphael B. Preventive intervention with the recently bereaved. *Arch Gen Psychiatry* 1977, 34: 1450–1454. (BIII)

This paper demonstrates that 'high-risk' bereaved people who receive counselling have fewer symptoms of lasting anxiety and tension than those who do not.

27 Murray Parkes C, Laungani P, Young B (eds). *Death and Bereavement Across Cultures*. London: Routledge, 1997. (AV)

28 *Inside Out: A Guide to Self-Management of Manic Depression*. London: Manic Depression Fellowship, 1995.

Available from The Manic Depression Fellowship 8–10 High Street, Kingston-upon-Thames, London KT1 1EY, UK. This advice is based on self-management training, 7–12 sessions of which have been shown to increase time between manic episodes. See Perry A, Tariner N, Morris R *et al*. Randomised control trial of efficacy of teaching patients with bipolar disorder to identify early symptoms of relapse and obtain treatment. *British Medical Journal* 1999, 318: 149–152.

29 Chou JC-Y. Recent advances in treatment of acute mania. *J Clin Psychopharm* 1991, 11: 3–21. (BII)

The authors conclude that antipsychotics are effective in mania, and they appear to have a more rapid effect than lithium.

30 Rifkin A, Doddi S, Karajgi B *et al*. Dosage of haloperidol for mania. *Br J Psych* 1994, 165: 113–116. (BII)

This paper concludes that doses of haloperidol over 10 mg a day in management of mania confer no benefit.

31   American Psychiatric Association. *Practice Guidelines: Bipolar Disorder*. Washington, DC, 1996. (AII)

This reviews four randomized control trials that show that benzodiazepines are effective, in place of, or in conjunction with, a neuroleptic, in sedating acutely agitated, manic patients.

32a   Cookson J. Lithium: balancing risks and benefits. *Br J Psychiatry* 1997, 171: 113–119. (BIII)

b   Dali I. Mania. *Lancet* 1997, 349: 1157–1160 .

c   Bowden C, Brugger A, Swann A *et al*. Efficacy of divolproex versus lithium and placebo in the treatment of mania. The Depakote Mania Study Group. *JAMA* 1994, 271: 918–924.

33   Zornberg G, Pope H Jr. Treatment of depression in bipolar disorder: new directions for research. *J Clin Psychopharmacol* 1993, 13: 397–408. (BIII)

Review of nine controlled studies shows high response rate to lithium for acute bipolar depression. Response may take six to eight weeks to become evident, however.

34a   Goodwin G. Lithium revisited: a re-examination of the placebo-controlled trials of lithium prophylaxis in manic-depressive disorder. *Br J Psychiatry* 1995, 167: 573–574. (BIII)

Trials show prophylactic use of lithium to be effective, although most trials have had methodological flaws.

b   Berghofer A, Kossmann B, Muller-Oerlinghausen B. Course of illness and pattern of recurrence in patients with affective disorders during long-term lithium prophylaxis: a retrospective analysis over 15 years. *Acta Psychiatr Scand* 1996, 93: 349–354.

The prophylactic effect of lithium can be maintained over at least 10 years.

35   See reference 31.

The upper limits of the therapeutic range for lithium is 1.0 meq/l. However, although the efficacy of lithium at 0.6–0.8 meq/l has not been formally studied, this is the range commonly chosen by patients and their doctors, as giving the best balance between effectiveness and side-effects.

36   Schou M. Effects of long-term lithium treatment on kidney function: an overview. *J Psychiatry* Res 1988, 22: 287–296.

A qualitative literature review.

37   Suppes T, Baldessanni RJ, Faedda GL. Risk of recurrence following discontinuation of lithium treatment in bipolar disorder. *Arch Gen Psych* 1991, 48: 1082–1088. (AIII)

38   Sachs G, Lafer B, Stoll A *et al*. A double-blind trial of bupropion versus desipramaine for bipolar depression. *J Clin Psychiatry* 1994, 55:391–393. (CII)

Preliminary evidence.

39   Reid S, Chalder T, Cleare A, Hotopf M, Wessely S. Chronic fatigue syndrome. In: *Clinical Evidence*, London: BMJ Pubs, 1999: 397–405. (BV)

40 Joyce J, Hotopf M, Wessely S. The prognosis of chronic fatigue and chronic fatigue syndrome: a systematic review. *Quart J Med* 1997: 90: 223–233. (BIV)

41 Price JR, Couper J. Cognitive behaviour therapy for CFS. Cochrane Library Issue 4, 1998. (AI)

42 Fulcher KY, White PD. A randomised controlled trial of graded exercise therapy in patients with the chronic fatigue syndrome. *BMJ* 1997, 314: 1647–1652. (AII)

43 See reference 39. (BIII)

44 Carette S, Bell MJ, Reynolds WJ *et al*. Comparison of amitriptyline, cyclobenzaprine, and placebo in the treatment of fibromyalgia. *Arthritis Rheum* 1994, 37: 32–40. (CII)

45 Hannonen P, Malminiemi K, Yli-Kerttula U *et al*. A randomised double-blind placebo controlled study of moclobemide and amitriptyline in the treatment of fibromyalgia in females without psychiatric disorder. *Br J Rheumatol* 1998, 37: 1279–1286. (CII)

46 Greden JF. Anxiety or caffeinism: a diagnosis dilemma. *Am J Psychiatry* 1974, 131: 1089–1092. (AV)

47 Wallin M, Rissanen A. Food and mood: relationship between food, serotonin and affective disorders. *Acta Psychiatr Scand* 1994, 377(Suppl): 36–40. (CV)
Quoted in *Guidelines for the Treatment and Management of Depression by Primary Health Care Professionals*. National Health Committee of New Zealand, 1996.

48 Hawton K, Kirk J. Problem-solving. In: Hawton K, Salkovskis PM, Kirk J, Clark DM (eds). *Cognitive Therapy for Psychiatric Problems: A Practical Guide*. Oxford: Oxford University Press, 1989. (AII)

49 Glenister D. Exercise and mental health: a review. *J Roy Soc Health* 1996, February: 7–13. (BIII)

50 McCann L, Holmes D. Influence of aerobic exercise on depression. *J Personal Social Psychol* 1984, 46: 1142–1147 (BIII)
Quoted in *Mental Health Promotion: a Quality Framework*. London: Health Education Authority, 1997.

51 Consensus, plus some, usually small, trials. For example, Donnan P, Hutchinson A, Paxton R *et al*. Self-help materials for anxiety: a randomised controlled trial in general practice. *Br J Gen Pract* 1990, 40: 498–501. (BV)
Audiotape and booklet is given to patients with chronic anxiety. Intervention led to reduced scores for depression, as well as for anxiety.

52 The differences in outcome between active drug and placebo are less in primary-care depressions than among more severe cases. (Clinical Practice Guideline Number 5: *Depression in Primary Care*. US Department of Health Human Services, Agency for Health Care Policy and Research, 1993; Treatment of Major Depression. AHCPR publication 93-0551.)
Fluoxetine does not produce better outcomes than tricyclic drugs in general primary-care depression (Simon G, VonKorff M, Heiligenstein J *et al*. Initial antidepressant

157

choice in primary care: effectiveness and cost of fluoxetine versus tricyclic antidepressants. *JAMA* 1996, 275: 1897–1902.)

Paroxetine and citalopram are both licensed for panic as well as depression, so may be useful where panic symptoms are prominent. Both selective serotonin re-uptake inhibitors and tricyclic antidepressants may initially worsen anxiety and panic symptoms, so should be introduced at low doses and slowly increased.

53a Linde K, Mulrow CD. St John's Wort for depression. Cochrane Library, Issue 1, 1999. (AI)

b Philip M, Kohnen R, Hiller K-O. Hypericum extract versus imipramine or placebo in patients with moderate depression: randomized, multi-centre study of treatment for eight weeks. *BMJ* 1999, 319: 1534–1539.

54 Thiede HM, Walper A. Inhibition of MAO and CoMT by hypericum extracts and hypericin. *J Geriat Psychiatr Neurol* 1994, 7(Suppl 1): S54–S56.

55 Interactions with tyramine-containing foods (eg beans, some cheeses, yeast, bovril, bananas, pickled herrings), are theoretically possible. However, there is, to date, an absence of spontaneous reports of these problems occurring.

56 Breckenbridge A. *Important Interactions Between St John's Wort (Hypericum perforata) Preparations and Prescribed Medicines.* Committee for Safety of Medicines, 29 February 2000.

Letter advises that hypericum reduces the therapeutic effect of indinavir, warfarin, cyclosporin, oral contraceptives, digoxin and theophylline, and may reduce the effect of other drugs — except topical medicines with limited systemic absorption and non-psychotropic medicines excreted renally. Adverse reactions may occur if combined with triptans (used to treat migraine) or SSRI antidepressants.

Information for professionals and the general public is available on the Medicines Control Agency website: URL: http://www.open.gov.uk/mca/mcahome.htm or by telephoning 020 7273 0000 (health professionals) or NHS Direct on 0845 46 47 (public).

57 McLean J, Pietroni P. Self care — who does best? *Soc Sci Med* 1990, 30(5): 591–596. (BIII)

This article describes a controlled trial of a general practice-based class teaching self-care skills, relaxation, stress management, medication, nutrition and exercise. Significant improvements were maintained after one year.

58 Catalan J, Gath DH, Anastasiades P *et al*. Evaluation of a brief psychological treatment for emotional disorders in primary care. *Psychol Med* 1991, 21: 1013–1018. (BII)

This paper describes a small randomized controlled trial. Patients receiving problem-solving therapy did significantly better than those receiving routine care. Patients were selected on the basis of higher symptom scores, however. Another group of patients with lower symptom scores, who were not treated, showed equal improvement to the treated group.

59 Gloaguen V, Cottraux J, Cucherat M *et al*. A meta-analysis of the effects on cognitive therapy in depressed patients. *J Affect Disord* 1998, 49: 59–72. (AI)

The studies supports cognitive therapy in patients with mild to moderate depression.

60   Sheldon T, Freemantle N, House A *et al*. Examining the effectiveness of treatments for depression in general practice. *J Mental Health* 1993, 2: 141–156. (BI)

This is a review of four randomized controlled trials that concluded that there is some evidence of effectiveness for cognitive therapy in depression in primary care, but that it is considerably weaker than cognitive therapy in major depressive disorder in secondary care.

61   Brown S. Excess mortality of schizophrenia: a meta-analysis. *Br J Psychiatry* 1997, 171: 502–508. (AI)

This article reports on life expectancy and excess mortality, including from physical illnesses, in patients with schizophrenia.

62   Adams CE, Eisenbruch M. Depot versus oral fluphenazine for those with schizophrenia. Cochrane Library, Issue 2, 1998. (AI)

63   Kendrick T, Millar E, Burns T, Ross F. Practice nurse involvement in giving depot neuroleptic injections: development of a patient assessment and monitoring checklist. *Prim Care Psychiatry* 1998, 4(3): 149–154. (AIV)

Of the 25% of people with schizophrenia who have no specialist contact, many have a practice nurse as their only regular professional contact. Levels of knowledge of schizophrenia and its treatment of those nurses was often no better than a lay persons.

64   Kemp R, Kirov G, Everitt B, David A. A randomised controlled trial of compliance therapy: 18 month follow up. *Br J Psychiatry* 1998, 172: 413–419. (AII)

Patients who received specific counselling regarding their attitudes towards their illness and drug treatment were five times more likely to take medication without prompting than controls.

65   Mari JJ, Streiner D. Family intervention for people with schizophrenia. The Cochrane Library, Issue 1, 1991. (AI)

Families receiving this intervention, which promotes a more supportive family environment, may expect the family member with schizophrenia to relapse less and to be in hospital less.

66   Jones C, Cormac I, Mota J, Campbell C. Cognitive behaviour therapy for schizophrenia. Cochrane Library, Issue 1, 1999. (AI)

Four small trials show that cognitive behaviour therapy is associated with substantially reduced risk of relapse.

67   Rabins PV. Psychosocial and management aspects of delirium. *Int Psychoger* 1991, 3(2): 319–324. (BV)

Reviews 21 papers. The evidence base is very thin.

68   Rummans TA, Evans JM, Krahn LE, Fleming KC. Delirium in elderly patients: evaluation and management. *Mayo Clinic Proc* 1995, 70(10): 989–998. (BV)

Reviews 55 papers. The evidence base is thin.

69   Eurodem Prevalence Research Group, Hofman PM, Rocca WA, Brayne C *et al*. The prevalence of dementia in Europe: a collaborative study of 1980–1999. *Int J Epidemiol* 1991, 20: 736–748.

70 Ballard C, Grace J, McKeith I *et al*. Neuroleptic sensitivity in dementia with Lewy bodies and Alzheimer's disease. *Lancet* 1998, 351: 1032–1033.

71a Stein K. *Donepezil in the Treatment of Mild to Moderate Dementia of the Alzheimer Type (SDAT)*. Report to the South and West Development and Evaluation Committee (DEC) no. 69. Bristol. NHS Executive, June 1997.

b Rogers SL, Farlow MR, Doody RS *et al*, and the Donepezil Study Group. *A Twenty Four Week, Double Blind, Placebo-Controlled Trial of Donepezil in Patients with Alzheimer's Disease. Neurology* 1998, 50: 136–145.

The limited number of studies available to date show that donepezil produces some improvement in a minority of patients with mild to moderate Alzheimer's disease (defined as those with a mini mental state examination score of between 10 and 26). There is no evidence to date that donepezil has any effect on the non-cognitive manifestations of Alzheimer's disease.

72 Martinsen E. Physical activity and major depressive disorder: clinical experience. *Acta Psychiatrica Scand* 1994, 377(Suppl): 23–27. (BIV)

This paper reviews 10 experimental studies which all indicate that aerobic exercise is more effective than no treatment for major depressive disorder.

73 Schuckit M. Alcohol and major depressive disorder: a clinical perspective *Acta Psychiatrica Scand* 1994, 377: 28–32. (AIV)

74 Schulberg H, Katon W, Simon G, Rush AJ. Best clinical practice: guidelines for managing major depression in primary care. *J Clin Psychiatry* 1999, 60(Suppl 7): 19–24. (BII)

This paper concludes that recovery rates for an acute episode of major depression in primary care are similar for guideline-driven pharmacotherapy and depression-specific psychotherapies, such as interpersonal therapy and problem-solving treatments. Medication takes four to six weeks to show effect and psychotherapies six to eight weeks.

75 Lave J, Frank R, Schulberg H, Kamlet M. Cost-effectiveness of treatments for major depression in primary care practice. *Arch Gen Psychiatry* 1998; 55(7): 645–651. (BII)

This paper describes a high-quality randomized controlled trial comparing standardized treatment by nortriptyline, interpersonal psychotherapy and primary physician's usual care (*n* >90 for each group) for major depression in primary care. Both standardized therapies were better than usual care, and more expensive. Those taking drugs did slightly better with respect to both quality of life and economic outcomes.

76 Paykel E, Hollyman J, Freeling P, Sedgwick P. Prediction of therapeutic benefit from amitriptyline in mild depression: a general practice, placebo-controlled trial. *J Affective Disord* 1988, 14: 83–95. (BIII)

Antidepressants don't show efficacy in mild acute depression. However, these is some evidence of efficacy in dysthemia (chronic, mild depressive syndrome that has been present for at least two years (Lima M, Moncrieff J. A comparison of drugs versus placebo for the treatment of dysthemia: a systematic review. Cochrane Database of Systematic Reviews, Depression, anxiety and neurosis module. Cochrane library, Issue 2, 1998).

77   NHS Centre for Reviews and Dissemination, University of York. The treatment of depression in primary care. *Effect Health Care* 1993, March(5): 1–12. (AII)

78   See reference 74.

Another conclusion from this paper is that recent randomized controlled trials conducted in primary care show a 50–60% response rate to all classes of antidepressants in primary-care patients.

79   Prien R, Kupfer D. Continuation drug therapy for major depressive episodes: how long should it be maintained? *Am J Psychiatry* 1986, 143; 18–23. (BII)

Concludes that patients treated for a first episode of uncomplicated depression, who respond well to an antidepressant, should receive a full therapeutic dose for at least 16–20 weeks after achieving full remission.

80   Reimherr F, Amsterdam J, Quitkin F *et al.* Optimal length of continuation therapy in depression: a prospective assessment during long-term fluoxetine treatment. *Am J Psychiatry* 1998, 155: 1247–1253. (BIII)

81   Kupfer D, Frank E, Perel J *et al.* Five-year outcomes for maintenance therapy: possible mechanisms and treatments. *J Clin Psychiatry* 1998; 59: 279–288.

This study was carried out by psychiatric patients. There are no comparable clinical trials of maintenance treatments' efficacy in reducing recurrence of depression in primary care.

82   Donaghue J, Taylor D. A review of the sub-optimal use of antidepressants in the treatment of depression. *CNS Drugs* 1999, In press. (BIII)

83a   DeRubeis RJ, Crits-Cristoph P. Empirically supported individual and group psychological treatments for adult mental disorders. *J Consulting Clin Psychol* 1998, 66(1): 37–52. (BI)

This work supports cognitive behaviour therapy, behaviour therapy and structured problem-solving. The studies reviewed are based in secondary care.

b   Schulberg HC, Bock MR, Madonia MJ *et al.* Treating major depression in primary care practice: eight month clinical outcomes. *Arch Gen Psychiatry* 1996, 53: 913–919. (BII)

This work supports interpersonal therapy.

c   Mynors-Wallis LM, Gath DH, Lloyd-Thomas AR, Tomlinson D. Randomised controlled trial comparing problem solving treatment with amitriptyline and placebo for major depression in primary care. *BMJ* 1995; 310: 441–445. (AII)

Where the therapies have been compared with each other, none appears clearly superior to the others. More variance in outcomes may be due to the strength of the therapeutic relationship rather than to the treatment method used. Problem-solving is the easiest therapy to learn and can be provided by GPs and primary-care nurses. Brief cognitive behaviour therapy is difficult to deliver, even using trained therapists (Scott C, Tacchi M, Jones R, Scott J. Abbreviated cognitive therapy for depression: a pilot study in primary care. *Behav Cogn Psychother* 1994, 22: 96–102), so the time taken is unlikely to be reduced below 8–10 hours (Scott J. Editorial: Psychological treatments for depression — an update. *Br J Psychiatry* 1995, 167: 289–292). Evidence for the effectiveness of therapies in depression in primary care tends to be weaker than in major depressive disorder in secondary care.

84 Thase M, Greenhouse J, Frank E *et al*. Treatment of major depression with psychotherapy or psychotherapy–pharmacotherapy combinations. *Arch Gen Psychiatry* 1997, 54: 1009–1015.

A Cochrane review on this topic is pending.

85 Evans M, Hollins S, De Rubeis R *et al*. Differential relapse following cognitive therapy and pharmacotherapy of depression. *Arch Gen Psychiatry* 1992, 49: 802–808.

86 Ostler KJ, Thompson C, Kinmonth ALK *et al*. The association between area socio-economic deprivation and depression among patients consulting in primary care. *Br J Psychiatry* 2000, In press.

Shows strong link between high indices of deprivation and poor prognosis for depression in primary care.

87 Kaltenbach K, Finnegan L. Children of maternal substance misusers. *Curr Opin Psychiatry* 1997, 10: 220–224.

Most harm caused is indirect, eg via ill health of mother, poor antenatal care or cigarette smoking. There is a smaller risk of direct harm caused by heroin — growth retardation — and cocaine and amphetamines.

88 Miller W, Rollnick S. *Motivational Interviewing: Preparing People to Change Addictive Behaviour*. New York: Guilford Press, 1991. (AV)

89 Gossop M, Stewart D, Marsden J. *NTORS at One Year: The National Treatment Outcome Research Study. Change in Substance Use, Health and Criminal Behaviour One Year After Intake*. London: Department of Health, 1998. (A1)

b Ward J, Mattick R, Hall W. *Maintenance Treatment and Other Opioid Replacement Therapies*. London: Harwood Academic Press, 1997.

c Jeffries V, Gabbay M, Carnwath T. Treatments for opiate users in primary care. Monograph for Enhancing Shared Care Project, Chapel Road, Sale, Manchester, M33 7FD. In press.

90 Lader M, Russel J. Guidelines for the prevention and treatment of benzodiazepine dependence: summary of a report from the Mental Health Foundation. *Addiction* 1993, 88(12): 1707–1708.

91 The Task Force to Review Services for Drug Misusers. *Report of an Independent Review of Drug Treatment Services in England*. London: DoH, 1995.

92 American Psychiatric Association. *Practice Guidelines: Substance Use Disorders*. Washington DC, 1996. (BII)

Reports a large randomized controlled trial replicated in a controlled trial comparing drug counselling, drug counselling plus supportive psychotherapy, and drug counselling plus cognitive behaviour therapy for methadone maintenance patients. Those with moderate to high depression or other psychiatric symptoms did better with either therapy in addition to drug counselling. For patients with low levels of psychiatric symptoms, all three treatments were equally effective.

93 Khantzian E. The primary care therapist and patient needs in substance abuse treatment. *Am J Drug Alcohol Abuse* 1988: 14: 159–167.

This paper reviews studies of relapse prevention through, for example, encouraging improved social and other relationships and activities.

94 Department of Health, The Scottish Office, The Welsh Office and DHSS Northern Ireland. *Drug Misuse and Dependence: Guidelines on Clinical Management*, 1999.

95 Although some patients may benefit from maintenance on low doses (eg 10–20 mg/day), in general, higher doses (>60 mg/day (range: 60–120 mg/day; average: 70–80 mg/day)) are associated with better outcome (Ball J, Ross A. *The Effectiveness of Methadone Maintenance Treatment*. New York: Springer–Verlag, 1991 (a prospective cohort study)). Doses for stabilization in withdrawal are also often above 60 mg/day and are determined by the patient's response, based on objective signs of withdrawal. (See reference 91).

96 Marsch LC. The efficacy of methadone maintenance interventions in reducing illicit opiate use, HIV risk behaviour and criminality: a meta-analysis. *Addiction* 1998, 93: 515–532. (A1)

97 Johnson R, Jaffe J, Fudala P. A controlled trial of beprenorphine treatment for opioid dependence *JAMA* 1992, 267: 2750–2755. (CIII)

Additional research is needed, particularly in a UK setting.

98 Bearn J, Gossop M, Strang J. Randomised double-blind comparison of lofexidine and methadone in the in-patient treatment of opiate withdrawal. *Drug Alcohol Depend* 1996, 43: 87–91. (BII)

Concludes that lofexidine is as efficacious as methadone.

99 Brown AS, Fleming PM. A naturalistic study of home detoxification from opiates using lofexidine. *J Psychopharmacol* 1998, 12: 93–96.

100 McLellan AT, Arndt IO, Metzger DS *et al*. The effects of psychosocial services in substance abuse treatment. *JAMA* 1993, 269: 1953–1959. (BII)

Patients who received employment help, psychiatric care and family therapy had better outcomes than those who received counselling, who in turn had better outcomes than those who received methadone only.

101 Imipramine, desipramine, trazodone and fluoxetine have all shown some efficacy. In the imipramine studies, most patients reduced their symptoms by at least half, and a third became free of symptoms. Higher doses of fluoxetine are needed than normally used for treating depression. Several trials of medication may be needed to establish the one most suitable for an individual patient. Fluoxetine is currently the only antidepressant licensed in the UK for bulimia nervosa. Selected references:

a Mitchell J, Raymond N, Specker S. A review of the controlled trials of pharmacotherapy and psychotherapy in the treatment of bulimia nervosa. *Int J Eating Disord* 1993, 15: 229–247. (BIII)

b American Psychiatric Association. *Practice Guidelines: Eating Disorders*. Washington DC, 1996. B(II)

102 Uncontrolled trials and one small controlled trial have suggested that fluoxetine may help some patients in the weight maintenance phases, but many patients do not improve with this or any other currently available medication. However, for patients with persistent depression, the use of antidepressants should be considered. Consider medication with fewer cardiovascular side-effects. Selected references:

a See reference 101b. (AIII)

b   Leach A. The psychopharmacotherapy of eating disorders. *Psychiatr Annals* 1995, 25: 628–633.

c   Kaye W, Gendall K, Strober M. Serotonin neuronal function and selective serotonin re-uptake inhibitor treatment in anorexia and bulimia nervosa. *Biol Psychiatr* 1998, 44: 825–838. (CIII)

103   Russell GFM, Szmukler GI, Dare C, Eisler I. An evaluation of family therapy in anorexia nervosa and bulimia nervosa. *Arch Gen Psychiatr* 1987, 44: 1047–1056. (CIII)

This paper shows that patients with anorexia nervosa with onset at or before age 18, and duration less than three years, did better with family therapy than individual therapy. Moreover, older patients did better with individual therapy. However, a major UK review, while supporting these recommendations, states that there are currently no high-quality reviews of psychological treatments for anorexia nervosa (see reference 59).

104   Whitbread J, McGown A. The treatment of bulimia nervosa: what is effective? A meta-analysis. *Int J Clin Psychol* 1994, 21: 32–44. (BI)

A Cochrane review is currently in progress.

105   Treasure J, Schmidt U, Troop N *et al.* First step in managing bulimia nervosa: controlled trial of a therapeutic manual. *BMJ* 1994, 308: 686–689. (BIII)

106   Shear K, Schulberg H. Anxiety disorders in primary care. *Bull Menninger Clinic* 1995, 59(2, Suppl A): 73–82. (BI)

This paper reviews studies of provision of psychoeducation and minimal interventions in primary care. Observations suggests that they show considerable promise as first-line interventions for anxiety disorders in primary care; however, more severely ill patients will require more sophisticated intervention.

107 See reference 12. (BII)

108a   Gould RA, Otto MW, Pollack MH, Yap L. Cognitive behavioural and pharmacological treatment of generalised anxiety disorder: a preliminary meta-analysis. *Behaviour Ther* 1997, 28(2): 285–305. (BI)

This paper revealed highest effect sizes for diazepam. Buspirone had a much lower effect size than either benzodiazepines or antidepressants, and its onset is slow (up to four weeks). However, problems with dependence and withdrawal are minimal compared with benzodiazepines.

b   Lader MH, Bond AJ. Interaction of pharmacological and psychological treatments of anxiety. *Br J Psychiatry* 1998, 173(Suppl 34): 165–168.

Firm conclusions are not possible. Observations suggests using benzodiazepines for treating anxiety initially, as these produce rapid symptomatic improvement; then psychological treatments can take over.

109   Imipramine and paroxetine have both been shown to reduce anxiety symptoms in the short term. Onset is slower than benzodiazepines but addiction is not a problem. Relapse rates following longer-term use are not known. Selected references (BII):

a   Kahn R, Mcnair D, Lipman R *et al.* Imipramine and chlordiazepoxide in depressive and anxiety disorders II. Efficacy in anxious out-patients. *Arch Gen Psychiatry* 1986, 43: 79–85.

b   Rocca P, Fonzo V, Scotta M *et al.* Paroxetine efficacy in the treatment of generalised anxiety disorder. *Acta Psychiatr Scand* 1997, 95: 444–450.

110 Tyrer P. Use of beta blocking drugs in psychiatry and neurology. *Drugs* 1980, 20: 300–308.

111 Gould RA, Otto MW, Pollack MH, Yap L. Cognitive behavioural and pharmacological treatment of generalised anxiety disorder: a preliminary meta-analysis. *Behaviour Ther* 1997, 28(2): 285–305. (BI)

Cognitive behavioural therapy (CBT) and anxiety management were found to be the most efficacious of psychological treatments. Medication and psychological therapies were equally efficacious in the short term. Gains of CBT and anxiety management were maintained at six months.

112 Kupshik G, Fisher C. Assisted bibliotherapy: effective, efficient treatment for moderate anxiety problems. *Br J Gen Pract* 1999, 49: 47–48. (BIII)

Learning self-help skills through reading, supported by contact with a clinician, lead to significant improvement of symptoms. Greater numbers improved with a greater amount of clinician contact, especially patients with less educational achievements.

113 See reference 57. (BIII)

114 Swinson RP, Soulios C, Cox BJ, Kuch K. Brief treatment of emergency-room patients with panic attacks. *Am J Psychiatry* 1992, 149: 944–946. (BIII)

People presenting to accident and emergency with panic provided with psychoeducation and exposure instructions had a significantly better outcome than controls.

115 American Psychiatric Association. Practice guideline for the treatment of patients with panic disorder. *Am J Psychiatry* 1998, 155(Suppl): 1–26. (AII)

Concludes that tricyclic antidepressants (TCAs), selective serotonin re-uptake inhibitors, monoamine oxidase inhibitors and benzodiazepines have roughly comparable efficacy in the short term. Benzodiazepines are useful in the very short term in situations where very rapid control of symptoms is critical. TCA side-effects may be problematic. Short-term use of medication commonly results in relapse, so longer-term use is recommended — 2–18 months — after which period, the relapse rate is not known).

116 Benzodiazepines are effective in many cases in suppressing panic in the short term. They are not an effective treatment for chronic panics or phobias, as there is no evidence that gains made continue when drugs are withdrawn; there is some evidence that they don't. Where patients are undergoing exposure therapy — ie dealing with the fear by gradually facing it — there is some evidence that benzodiazepines may actually interfere with maintaining longer-term therapeutic gains.

Selected references (BII):

a American Psychiatric Association. Practice guideline for the treatment of patients with panic disorder. *Am J Psychiatry* 1998, 155(Suppl): 1–26.

b Marks I, Swinson P, Basoglu M *et al*. Alprazolam and exposure alone and combined in panic disorder with agoraphobia. A controlled study in London and Toronto. *Br J Psychiatry* 1993, 162: 776–787.

117 See reference 13a

The authors conclude that 85% of chronic patients stay well between the one- and two-year follow-up, when treated using cognitive behaviour therapy.

118 Marks I, Swinson RP. Alprazolam and exposure for panic disorder with agoraphobia; summary of London/Toronto results. *J Psychiatric Res* 1990, 24: 100–101. (AII)

Where agoraphobic fear and avoidance is present, with panic, exposure — a behavioural treatment — proved to be twice as effective as alprazolam.

119 Wade WA, Treat TA, Stuart GL. Transporting an empirically supported treatment for panic disorder to a service clinic setting; a benchmarking strategy. *J Consult Clin Psychol* 1998, 66: 231–239. (CIII)

120 Murray B, Stein M, Michael R *et al*. Paroxetine treatment of generalized social phobia (social anxiety disorder): a randomised controlled trial. *JAMA* 1998, 280: 8. (CII)

Symptoms improved in short term — ie 11-week trial). However, relapse rates are very high after discontinuation, and relapse rates after longer-term treatment are not known. (See Stein MB, Chartier MJ, Hazen Al *et al*. Paroxetine in the treatment of generalised social phobia: open-label treatment and double-blind, placebo-controlled discontinuation. *J Clin Psychopharmacol* 1996, 16: 218–222.)

121 DeRubeis RJ, Crits-Cristoph P. Empirically supported individual and group psychological treatments for adult mental disorders. *J Consult Clin Psychol* 1998, 66(1): 37–52. (AII)

Exposure with cognitive therapy shows efficacy for social phobia; exposure with cognitive behaviour therapy shows efficacy for agoraphobia.) Efficacy of exposure behaviour therapy has proven twice that of alprazolam for agoraphobic fear and avoidance (see reference 118).

122 Fichtner C, Poddig B, deVito R. Post-traumatic stress disorder: pathophysiological aspects and pharmacological approaches to treatment. *CNS Drugs* 1997, 8(4): 293–322. (CII)

The research base is limited. There is evidence of only limited efficacy for a wide range of drugs. Fluoxetine is the most widely studied selective serotonin re-uptake inhibitor. Phenelzine appears more effective than tricyclic antidepressants (TCAs) for re-experiencing symptoms. The most studied TCAs were imipramine and amitriptyline.

123 See reference 13a.

Concludes that effective treatments appear to involve relatively complex combinations of cognitive techniques and exposure and may best be administered by staff specializing in this disorder.

124 Foa EB, Meadows EA. Psychosocial treatments for post-traumatic stress disorder: a critical review. *Ann Rev Psychology* 1997, 48: 449–480. (BII)

It shows that exposure — a behavioural treatment — and supportive counselling are equally effective at the end of treatment, but exposure is superior after three months.

125 Boolell M, Gepi-Atee S, Gingell C, Allen MK. Sildenafil: a novel effective oral therapy for male erectile dysfunction. *Br J Urol* 1996, 78: 257–261. (AII)

126 Padma-Nathan H, Hellstrom WJG, Kaiser RE *et al*. Treatment of men with erectile dysfunction with transurethral alprostadil. *New Engl J Med* 1997, 336: 1–7. (AII)

127 Linet OI, Ogrine FG. Efficacy and safety of intracavernosal alprostadil in men with erectile dysfunction. *New Engl J Med* 1996, 334: 873–877. (AII)

128 McClusky HY, Milby JB, Switzer PK *et al*. Efficacy of behavioural versus triazolam treatment in persistent sleep-onset insomnia. *Am J Psychiatry* 1991, 148: 121–126. (BVplus)

This small trial found that triazolam had an immediate effect on persistent insomnia, and behavioural treatment took three weeks to have an equivalent effect. Behavioural treatment is more effective at one-month follow-up.

129 Eisen J, MacFarlane J, Shapiro C. Psychotropic drugs and sleep. *BMJ* 1993, 306: 1331–1334.

130 Rasmussen P. A role of phytotherapy in the treatment of benzodiazepines and opiate drug withdrawal. *Eur J Herbal Med* 1997, 3(1): 11–21. (CIV)

Quoted in: Wallcraft J. *Healing Minds: A Report on Current Research, Policy and Practice Concerning the Use of Complementary and Alternative Therapies for a Wide Range of Mental Health Problems*. Mental Health Foundation, 1998. (Refers to trials — some in animals — showing that valerian can improve the quality of sleep, and without a hangover effect the next day. No studies of the long-term safety of valerian have been reported. The effect on sleep is weak.

131 Bootzin R, Perlis M. Non-pharmacological treatments of insomnia. *J Clin Psychiatry* 1992, 53(6 Suppl): 37–40.

This review found sleep hygiene training during individual counselling and stimulus control instructions are more effective than relaxation training.

132 WHO. *Insomnia: Behavioural and Cognitive Interventions*. Geneva: Division of Mental Health, 1993.

133 Goldberg R, Dennis H, Novack M, Gask L. The recognition and management of somatization: what is needed in primary care training. *Psychosomatics* 1992, 33(1): 55–61. (BV)

134 Smith GR, Rost K, Kashner M. A trial of the effect of a standardised psychiatric consultation on health outcomes and costs in somatising patients. *Arch Gen Psych* 1995, 52(3): 238–243. (BII)

135 Fishbain DA, Cutler RB, Rosomoff HL, Rosomoff RS. Do antidepressants have an analgesic effect in psychogenic pain and somatoform pain disorder? A meta-analysis. *Psychosom Med* 1998, 60(4): 503–509. (B1)

136 Pilowsky I, Barrow C. A controlled study of psychotherapy and amitriptyline used individually and in combination in the treatment of chronic intractable psychogenic pain. *Pain* 1990, 40: 3–19. (CIII)

137a Speckens A, Van Hemert A, Spinhoven P *et al*. Cognitive behavioural therapy for medically unexplained physical symptoms: a randomized controlled trial. *BMJ* 1995, 311: 1328–1332. (BII)

Six to 16 sessions of cognitive behaviour therapy were conducted in medical outpatients. Intervention was found to be effective and acceptable to patients, and gains were maintained at 12-month follow-up.

167

b   Kashner TM, Rost K, Cohen B *et al*. Enhancing the health of somatization disorder patients: effectiveness of short-term group therapy. *Psychosomatics* 1995, 36: 924–932. (BII)

Random controlled trial of 70 patients in primary care offered eight sessions of group therapy. Improvements, both physical and emotional, were maintained at one year.

c   Guthrie E. Emotional disorder in chronic illness: psychotherapeutic interventions. *Br J Psychiatry* 1996, 168(3): 265–273.

This review includes eight studies of somatic presentation of psychological problems. Two studies show cognitive behaviour therapy to be effective in atypical chest pain and functional dyspepsia, and hypnosis to be effective in two studies for irritable bowel syndrome. Compliance is poor, however. Patients with a long history of symptoms and marked abnormal illness behaviour are unlikely to respond to a brief intervention

Acknowledgements

The primary care classification of mental disorders would not have been possible without the advice, support and collaboration of primary-care workers, researchers, WHO Collaborating Centres and other agencies. WHO wishes to express its particular thanks to the following for their valuable collaboration:

International version
J Banda (Zambia), D Berardi (Italy), A Bertelsen (Denmark), E Busnello (Brazil), A Carla (France), J E Cooper (UK), N Dedeoglu (Turkey), M P Deva (Malaysia), D Goldberg (UK), M Gomel (Australia), O Gureje (Nigeria), C Hunt (Australia), R Jenkins (UK), S Murthy (India), K Ogel (Turkey), C Pull (Luxembourg), D Roy (Canada), G E Simon (USA), P Verta (France), M Von Korff (USA) and N Wig (India).

D Goldberg and G E Simon were chief consultants for the project and compiled the information for each category of disorder.

Overall management and coordination of the project was carried out by Dr T B Ustun.

World Organization of National Colleges and Academies and Academic Associations of General Practitioners/Family Physicians (WONCA):
C Bridges-Webb and H Lamberts.

World Psychiatric Association:
N Sartorius and J J López-Ibor Jr.

National Institute of Mental Health, USA
K Magruder, D Regier, J Gonzales and G Norquist.

Bristol version
The editorial team were Catherine Crilly, Jonathan Evans, Glynn Harrison, Gemma McCann, Debbie Sharp, Cameron Smith, Ellen Wilkinson. Brendan Blair assisted with the guide to the Mental Health Act.

UK version
Expert input on particular topics was generously provided by the following people:

Dr Sube Banerjee, Dr Tom Carnwath, Professor Anna Cooper, Dr Michael Crow, Dr Katy Drummond, Dr Jim Dyer, Dr Mike Farrell, Dr Mark Gabbay, Dr Clare Garrada, Dr Linda Gask, Professor Sir David Goldberg, Professor Sheila Hollins, Dr Gundi Kiemle, Professor Tony Kendrick, Professor Malcolm Lader, Professor Alistair MacDonald, Professor Isaac Marks, Mr John Park, Mr Stephen Popplestone, Ms Sue Plummer, Professor Jan Scott, Dr Ulrike Schmidt , Dr James Strachan, Mr David Taylor, Dr Andre Tylee, Dr John Turvill, Professor Simon Wessely. Jo Paton researched the evidence base and compiled the references and notes section and adapted the patient information leaflets. Lynette Timms checked all the contact details for the Community Resources.

UK National Editorial Team
David Goldberg, Linda Gask, Rachel Jenkins, Barry Lewis, Jo Paton, Debbie Sharp, André Tylee. Overall management and coordination of the project was carried out by Jo Paton, under the direction of Professor Rachel Jenkins.

UK National Consensus Group
Mrs Elizabeth Armstrong, Director, National Depression Care Training Centre; Dr Sube Banerjee, Lecturer Institute of Psychiatry; Dr Mary Burd, Primary Care Psychology and Counselling Service; Dr Richard Bynge, Lecturer, Department of General Practice and Primary Care, UMDS; Professor Anna Cooper, Professor of Psychiatry of Learning Disability, Glasgow University; Dr Katie Drummond, Psychiatrist of Disability; Ms Joan Foster, Chair, Counsellors in Primary Care; Dr Mark Gabbay, Senior Lecturer, Department of General Practice, Liverpool University; Dr Clare Garrada, RCGP Mental Health Task Force and Senior Policy Advisor, Department of Health; Dr Linda Gask, Reader in Psychiatry, University of Manchester; Professor Sir David Goldberg, Professor of Psychiatry, Institute of Psychiatry; Professor Glynn Harrison, Professor of Psychiatry, Bristol University; Professor Sheila Hollins, Department of Psychiatry of Disability, St. George's Hospital; Professor Rachel Jenkins, Director, WHO Collaborating Centre for Research and Training for Mental Health; Professor Tony Kendrick, Professor of General Practice, University of Southampton; Dr David Kessler, GP, PriMHE; Professor Malcolm Lader, Professor of Clinical Psychopharmacology, Institute of Psychiatry; Dr Chris Manning, GP, co-Chair PriMHE; Dr Richard Maxwell, GP, PriMHE; Ms Sue Plummer, Research Nurse, Department of Psychiatric Nursing, Institute of Psychiatry; Professor Debbie Sharp, Professor of

General Practice, University of Bristol; Professor Simon Wessley, Institute of Psychiatry; Dr Ellen Wilkinson, Lecturer, Department of Mental Health, Bristol University; Dr Alastair Wright, GP, formerly Editor, *British Journal of General Practice*; Ms Jo Paton, Researcher, Institute of Psychiatry.

Commenters
The following people also provided valuable comments: Marion Beeforth, Service User; Nigel Duerdoth, Mental Health Foundation; John Mellor Clark, Psychological Therapies Research Centre; Dr Peter Orton, GP Advisor, Royal Society of Medicine; Dr Salman Rawaf, Public Health Department, MSW Health Authority; Ms Jackie Carnell, General Secretary, Community Practitioners and Health Visitors Association; Ms Jo Hesketh, Director, The Queens Nursing Institute; Ms Karen Gupta, Chair, Practice Nurse Forum, Royal College of Nursing; Mr Ian Moore, Community Mental Health Team Association; Brian Rodgers, Community Psychiatric Nurse Assocation.

Permissions
We are grateful to the following organizations who kindly granted copyright permission for us to reproduce or adapt their work:
The World Health Organization Division of Mental Health and Substance Abuse — material from *Mental Disorders in Primary Care; a WHO Educational Package* — patient leaflets numbers 3-2, 4, 6, 7, 11 and 12, all the interactive summary cards and the diagnostic checklist.
World Health Organization Collaborating Centres in Mental Health, Sydney and London: extracts from Andrews G, Jenkins R (eds). *Management of Mental Disorders*, UK Edition. Sydney: World Health Organization Collaborating Centre for Mental Health and Substance Abuse, 1999 — used in patient leaflets numbers 1, 2, 3, 5, 6, 8-2, 9, 10 and 11 and the Social and living skills checklist (13-4).
Mental Health Foundation: Extract from *Managing Anxiety and Depression: a Self-Help Guide*, used in patient leaflet 1-2.
Nottingham Alcohol and Drug Team: extract from *Problem Drug Use*, used in patient leaflet 8-1.
Chronic Fatigue Syndrome Research Unit, GKT School of Medicine, London: material from Patient Management Package used in patient leaflets 6-2 and 6-3.

This Guide has been endorsed by the following groups:

- The Royal College of General Practitioners' Unit for Mental Health Education in Primary Care
- The Royal College of Psychiatrists
- The Royal College of Nursing
- The Patients' Association
- Primary care Mental Health Education (PriMHE)
- The Association of Primary Care Counsellors
- The Community Practitioners' and Health Visitors' Association
- The Queens Nursing Institute
- The Community Psychiatric Nurse Association
- The Depression Care Training Centre.

Interactive summary cards

The six pages that follow contain summaries of information about the six disorders most common in primary care.

These are designed to be used interactively within the consultation, to help the practitioner explain key features of the disorder to the patient and enter into discussion about a possible management plan. They are also contained on the disc and can be printed out and mounted on either side of a piece of A4 card for ease of use.

Mental health in primary care
Alcohol problems

There is one unit of alcohol in:
½ pint of ordinary strength beer, lager or cider
¼ pint of extra strength beer, lager or cider
1 small glass of white (8 or 9% ABV) wine
2/3 small glass of red (11 or 12% ABV) wine
1 single measure of spirits (30 ml)

Common symptoms

'High-risk' drinking:
Men
More than three units
alcohol/day
(21 units/week)

Women
More than two units
alcohol/day
(14 units/week)

**Many have no
symptoms but
are at risk**

Psychological:
→ Poor concentration
→ Sleep problems
→ Less able to think
   clearly
→ Depression
→ Anxiety/stress

Physical:
→Hangovers/blackouts
→ Injuries
→ Tiredness/lack
   of energy
→ Weight gain
→ Poor coordination
→ High blood pressure
→ Impotence
→ Vomiting/nausea
→ Gastritis/diarrhoea
→ Liver disease
→ Brain damage

→ Difficulties and arguments with family/friends
→ Difficulties performing at work/home
→ Withdrawal from friends and social activities
→ Legal problems.

Alcohol problems are treatable
Alcohol problems *do not* mean weakness
Alcohol problems *do not* mean you are a bad person
Alcohol problems *do* mean that you have a medical problem or a lifestyle
problem.

What treatments can help?
Both therapies are most often needed:

Supportive therapy:
→ to reduce drinking
→ to stop drinking
→ for stress
→ for prevention of life problems
→ for education of the family members
   for support.

Medication:
→ for moderate to severe withdrawal
→ for physical problems
→ consider for relapse prevention.

Set goals: acceptable levels of drinking

Who?	How many drinks?	How often?
Men	No more than three units	Each day (only for five days/week)
Women	No more than two units	Each day (only for five days/week)

Have two non-alcohol drinking days/week.

Keep in mind: the less the person drinks, the better it is.

➡ Pregnancy
➡ Physical alcohol dependence
➡ Physical problems made worse by drinking
➡ Driving, biking
➡ Operating machinery
➡ Exercising (swimming, jogging, etc.)

➡ Recommendation is not to drink

Determine action: how to reach target levels

➡ Keep track of your alcohol consumption
➡ Turn to family and/ or friends for support
➡ Have one or more non-alcoholic drinks before each drink
➡ Delay the time of day that you drink
➡ Take smaller sips

➡ Engage in alternative activities at times that you would normally drink (eg when you are feeling bored or stressed)
➡ Switch to low alcoholic drinks
➡ Decide on non-drinking days (2 days or more per week)

➡ Eat before starting to drink
➡ Join a support group
➡ Quench your thirst with non-alcoholic drinks
➡ Avoid or reduce time spent with heavy-drinking friends
➡ Avoid bars, cafes or former drinking places.

Review progress: are you keeping on track?

Questions to ask:
➡ Am I keeping to my goals?
➡ What are the difficult times?
➡ Am I losing motivation?
➡ Do I need more help?

Progress tips:
➡ Every week, record how much you drink over the week
➡ Avoid these difficult situations or plan activities to help you cope with them
➡ Think back to your original reasons for cutting down or stopping
➡ Come back for help, talk to family and friends.

Mental health in primary care
Anxiety

Common symptoms

Psychological:
→ Tension
→ Worry
→ Panic
→ Feelings of unreality
→ Fear of going crazy
→ Fear of dying
→ Fear of losing control

Physical:
→ Trembling
→ Sweating
→ Heart pounding
→ Light headedness
→ Dizziness

→ Muscle tension
→ Nausea
→ Breathlessness
→ Numbness
→ Stomach pains
→ Tingling sensation

→ **Disruptive to work, social or family life** ←

Anxiety disorders are common and treatable
Anxiety *does not* mean weakness
Anxiety *does not* mean losing the mind
Anxiety *does not* mean personality problems
Severe anxiety *does* mean a disorder which requires treatment.

Common forms of anxiety

Generalized anxiety disorder:
→ persistent/ excessive worry
→ physical symptoms.

Panic disorder:
→ sudden intense fear
→ physical symptoms
→ psychological symptoms.

Social phobia:
→ Fear/avoidance social situations
→ fear of being criticized
→ physical symptoms
→ psychological symptoms.

Agoraphobia:
→ Fear/avoidance of situations where escape is difficult
→ leaving familiar places alone
→ physical symptoms
→ psychological symptoms.

What treatments can help?
Both therapies are most often needed:

Supportive therapy for:
→ slow breathing/relaxation
→ exposure to feared situations
→ realistic/positive thinking
→ problem-solving.

Medication:
→ for severe anxiety
→ for panic attacks.

Anxiety

About medication

Short term
➡ use for severe anxiety
➡ can be addictive and
   ineffective when used in
   the long term

Side-effects
➡ are important to report

Counselling
➡ (emotional support and
   problem-solving) is always
   recommended with medication

Ongoing review
➡ of medication use
   is recommended.

Slow breathing to reduce physical symptoms of anxiety

➡ Breath in for three seconds and out for three seconds, and pause for three seconds before breathing in again.
➡ Practise 10 minutes morning or night (five minutes is better than nothing).
➡ Use before and during situations that make you anxious.
➡ Regularly check and slow down breathing throughout the day.

Change attitudes and ways of thinking

'My chest is hurting and I can't breathe, I must be having a heart attack.'

Instead: 'I am having a panic attack, I should slow my breathing down and I will feel better.'

'I hope they don't ask me a question, I won't know what to say.'

Instead: 'Whatever I say will be OK, I am not being judged. Others are not being judged, why should I be?'

'My partner has not called as planned. Something terrible must have happened.'

Instead: 'They might not have been able to get to a phone. It is very unlikely that something terrible has happened.'

Exposure to overcome anxiety and avoidance

Easy stage ➡ Moderate stage ➡ Hard stage
(eg walking on own)   (eg lunch with a friend)   (eg shopping with a friend)

➡ Use slow breathing to control anxiety
➡ Do not move to the next stage until anxiety decreases to an acceptable level.

Mental health in primary care
Chronic tiredness

Common symptoms

Compared with previous level of energy, and compared to people known to you:

Tired all the time   Tire easily   Tired despite rest

➡ Disruptive to work, social and family life
➡ Affects ability to carry out routine and other tasks
➡ Feelings of frustration.

Chronic Fatigue Syndrome is a much rarer condition, diagnosed when substantial physical and mental fatigue lasts longer than six months and there are no significant findings on physical or laboratory investigation.

Common triggers

Psychological triggers:
➡ Depression ➡ Doing too
➡ Stress   much
➡ Worry   activity
➡ Anxiety.   ➡ Doing too
                   little
                   activity.

Physical triggers:
➡ Anaemia   ➡ Thyroid
➡ Bronchitis   disorder
➡ Asthma   ➡ Influenza
➡ Diabetes   ➡ Alcohol/
➡ Arthritis.   drug use
                  ➡ Bacterial,
                     viral and
                     other
                     infections.

Medication:
➡ Steroids
➡ Antihistamines.

What treatments can help?

Both therapies are most often needed:

Supportive therapy for:
➡ depression
➡ worry/anxiety
➡ stress/life problems
➡ lifestyle change
➡ level of physical activity.

Medication:
➡ for other mental or physical disorders
➡ anti-depressants are sometimes useful
➡ there are no effective medications specific to fatigue and the main treatment follows psychological lines.

Behavioural strategies

➡ Examine how well you are sleeping.
➡ Have a brief rest period of about 2 weeks, in which there are no extensive activities.
➡ After the period of brief rest, gradually return to your usual activities.

➡ Plan pleasant/enjoyable activities into your week.
➡ Gradually build up a regular exercise routine.
➡ Do not push yourself too hard; remember to build up all activities gradually and steadily.

➡ Try to have regular meals during the day.
➡ Try to keep to a healthy diet.
➡ Use relaxation techniques, for example, slow breathing.

Slow breathing for relaxation

➡ Breath in for three seconds
➡ Breath out for three seconds
➡ Pause for three seconds before breathing in again
➡ Practise for 10 minutes at night (five minutes is better than nothing).

Increase level of physical activity

A little activity **one or two times a week** (eg walking)	**Daily activities —** **not much effort** (eg fast walking, shopping, cleaning)	**Activity that makes** **you out of breath for** **20 minutes or more,** **three to five times a week** (eg jogging)
Inactive	**Some activity**	**Active**

Mental health in primary care
Depression

Common symptoms

Mood and motivation:
- Continuous low mood
- Loss of interest or pleasure
- Hopelessness
- Helplessness
- Worthlessness

Psychological:
- Guilt/negative attitude to self
- Poor concentration/ memory
- Thoughts of death or suicide
- Tearfulness

Physical:
- Slowing down or agitation
- Tiredness/lack of energy
- Sleep problems
- Disturbed appetite (weight loss/increase)

- Difficulties carrying out routine activities
- Difficulties performing at work
- Difficulties with home life
- Withdrawal from friends and social activities.

Depression is common and treatable
- Depression *does not* mean weakness
- Depression *does not* mean laziness
- Depression *does mean* that you have a medical disorder which requires treatment.

Common triggers

Psychological:
Major life events, eg
- Recent bereavement
- Relationship problems
- Unemployment
- Moving house
- Stress at work
- Financial
- problems.

Other:
- Family history of depression
- Childbirth
- Menopause
- Seasonal changes
- Chronic medical conditions
- Alcohol and substance use disorders.

Illness:
- Infectious diseases
- Influenza hepatitis.

Medication:
- Antihypertensives
- H2 blockers
- Oral contraceptives
- Corticosteroids.

What treatments can help?

Both therapies are most often needed:

Supportive therapy for:
- stress/life problems
- patterns of negative thinking
- prevention of further episode.

Medication:
- for depressed mood or loss of interest/ pleasure for two or more weeks and at least four of the symptoms mentioned earlier
- for little response to supportive therapy (counselling)
- for recurrent depression
- for a family history of depression.

About medication

Effective
Usually works faster than other methods.

Treatment plan
must be strictly adhered to.

Drugs
➡ are not addictive
➡ interact in a harmful way with alcohol
➡ improvement takes time, generally three weeks for a response
➡ do not take in combination with St John's wort.

Side-effects
must be reported, but generally start improving within 7–10 days.

Progress
➡ same medication should continue
➡ unless a different decision is taken by the doctor
➡ medication should not be discontinued without doctor's knowledge in case a drug is not effective, another drug may be tried.

Time period
Medication to be continued at least four to six months after initial improvement.

Ongoing review
is necessary over the next few months.

Increase time spent on enjoyable activities

➡ Set small achievable, daily goals for doing pleasant activities
➡ Plan time for activities and increase the amount of time spent on these each week

➡ Plan things to look forward to in future
➡ Keep busy even when it is hard to feel motivated
➡ Try to be with other people/family members.

Problem-solving plan

Discuss
problems with partner/family members, trusted friend or counsellor.

Distance
yourself to look at problems as though you were an observer.

Options
Work out possible solutions to solve the problems.

Pros and cons
Examine advantages and disadvantages of each option.

Set a time frame
to examine and resolve problems.

Make an action plan
for working through the problems over a period of time.

Review
Progress made in solving problems.

Change attitudes and way of thinking

'I will always feel this way; things will never change.'

Instead: 'These feelings are temporary. With treatment, things will look better in a few weeks.'

'It's all my fault. I do not seem to be able to do anything right.'

Instead: 'These are negative thoughts that are the result of depression. What evidence for this do I really have?'

Mental health in primary care
Sleep problems

Common symptoms

➡ Difficulty falling asleep
➡ Frequent awakening

➡ Early morning awakening
➡ Restless or unrefreshing sleep

➡ Difficulties at work and in social and family life
➡ Makes it difficult to carry out routine or desired tasks.

Common causes

Psychological:	Physical: Medical problems:	Lifestyle:	Environmental:
➡ Depression	➡ Overweight	➡ Too hot or too cold	➡ Noise
➡ Anxiety	➡ Heart failure	➡ Tea, coffee and alcohol	➡ Pollution
➡ Worries	➡ Nose, throat and lung disease	➡ Heavy meal before sleep	➡ Lack of privacy
➡ Stress.	➡ Sleep apnoea	➡ Daytime naps	➡ Over-crowding.
	➡ Narcolepsy	➡ Irregular sleep schedule.	
	➡ Pains.		
	Medications:		
	➡ Steroids		
	➡ Decongestants		
	➡ Others.		

What treatments can help?

Supportive therapy is the preferred treatment

Supportive therapy for:
➡ stress/life problems
➡ depression
➡ worry
➡ changes in lifestyle and sleep habits.

Medication:
➡ for temporary sleep problems
➡ for short term use in chronic problems to break sleep cycle.

About medication

Short term
➡ use for short period of time.

Long-term
➡ when used in the long term, there may be difficulties stopping, leading to dependence.

Side-effects
➡ are important to report.

Harmful
➡ when alcohol and other drugs are used.

Ongoing review
➡ of medication use is recommended.

Lifestyle change strategies

➡ Try to minimize noise in your sleep environment, if necessary consider ear plugs.
➡ Try to make sure that the room in which you are sleeping is not too hot or cold.
➡ Reduce the amount of alcohol, coffee and tea that you drink, especially in the evenings.

➡ Try to avoid eating immediately before going to sleep.
➡ Try to have your dinner earlier in the evening, rather than later.
➡ Don't lie in bed trying sleep. Get up and do something relaxing until you feel tired.
➡ Have regular times for going to bed at night and waking up in the morning.

➡ Reduce mental and physical activity during the evenings.
➡ Increase your level of physical activity during the day; build up a regular exercise routine.
➡ Avoid daytime naps, even if you have not slept the night before.
➡ Use relaxation techniques, for example, slow breathing.

Slow breathing for relaxation

➡ Breath in for three seconds
➡ Breath out for three seconds
➡ Pause for three seconds before breathing in again
➡ Practise for 10 minutes at night (five minutes is better than nothing).

More evaluation may be needed:
➡ if someone stops breathing during sleep (sleep apnoea)
➡ if there is a daytime sleepiness without possible explanation.

Mental health in primary care
Unexplained somatic complaints

Common, unexplained physical problems

- Headaches
- Chest pains
- Difficulty in breathing
- Difficulty in swallowing

- Nausea
- Vomiting
- Abdominal pain
- Lower back pain

- Skin rashes
- Frequent urination
- Diarrhoea
- Skin and muscle discomfort.

Associated worries and concerns

- Associated symptoms and problems
- Beliefs (about what is causing the symptoms)
- Fear (of what might happen).

Physical symptoms are real

A vicious circle can develop:
- Emotional stress can cause physical symptoms or make them worse.
- Physical symptoms can lead to more emotional stress.
- Emotional stress can make physical symptoms worse.

Headaches Difficulty in swallowing Chest pain/difficulty in breathing Abdominal pain/nausea/vomiting Frequent urination/diarrhoea/impotence Skin rashes	may all be caused or made worse by stress, anxiety worry, anger, depression

What treatments can help?

Supportive treatment most often needed:

- Effective reassurance, after history and detailed physical examination.
- Management of stress/life problems.
- Treatment of associated depression, anxiety, alcohol problems.
- Learning to relax.
- Avoiding patterns of negative thinking.
- Increasing levels of physical activity.
- Increasing positive/pleasurable activities.

Unexplained somatic complaints

Useful strategies

Reassurance
→ Stress often produces physical symptoms or makes them worse.
→ There are no signs of serious illness.
→ You can benefit from learning strategies to reduce the impact of your symptoms.

Slow breathing to reduce common physical symptoms
(eg muscle tension, hot and cold flushes, headaches, chest tightness)
→ Breath in for three seconds and out for three seconds and pause for three seconds before breathing in again.
→ Practise 10 minutes morning or night (five minutes is better than nothing).
→ Use before and during situations that make you anxious.
→ Regularly check and slow down breathing throughout the day.

Change attitudes and way of thinking

'I can't understand why the tests are negative. I feel the pain; it is probably something really unusual that I have.'

Instead: 'The pain is real, but I've been checked out physically and I have had all the relevant tests. Many other things, such as worry and stress, can cause these pains.'

'Maybe my doctor has missed something. I should try another doctor or better still a specialist instead.'

Instead: 'It is very unlikely that these doctors have missed something. It is unlikely that a specialist would say anything different. Maybe I should examine whether stress, tension, or my lifestyle is contributing to the pain.'

'Why won't this pain go away. I'm not feeling well; I've probably got cancer.'

Instead: 'This is not the first time that I've thought that there was *something* terribly *wrong* and *in fact* nothing serious developed. I should learn to relax and focus my thoughts on other things to distract myself from the pains.'

Increase level of physical activity

A little activity one or two times a week (eg walking)	**Daily activities —** not much effort (eg fast walking, shopping, cleaning)	**Activity that makes** you out of breath for 20 minutes or more, three to five times a week (eg jogging)
↓	↓	↓
Inactive	Some activity	Active

Index

acamprosate 26
adjustment disorder (F43.2) 19–21
  counselling 20
  diagnosis 19
  differential diagnosis 19–20
  information for patients and
      family 20, 21
  medication 20
  referral 20
adolescents
  depression 59
  resources 123
agitation, control 17
agoraphobia 79–81
akathisia 45–6
alcohol misuse (F10) 22–7, 39, 40,
    43, 44, 55, 174–5
  action determination 173
  advice/support to patient and
      family 23–5
  anxiety 26
  blood tests 23
  counselling 26
  dependence 22–3
  depression 26, 59
  detoxification 25, 26
  diagnostic features 22–3
  differential diagnosis 23
  drug use disorders 63
  eating disorders 68, 70
  goal setting 175
  harmful 22
  information for patient and
      family 23, 27, 120–1
  medication 25–6
  Mental Health (Scotland) Act
      (1984) 113
  post-traumatic stress
      disorder 82
  presentation 22
  progress review 175
  referral 26
  resources for patients and
      families 27, 120–1, 133
  symptoms 172
  treatment 172
Alzheimer's disease 50, 53

amitriptyline 97
anorexia nervosa 67–70
  resources 127
anorgasmia 87
anti-anxiety medication 17
  panic disorder 77
  phobic disorders 81
anticholinesterase drugs 53
antidepressants 57–8
  anxiety 73
  anxiety and depression 41
  bipolar disorder 33–4
  bulimia 69
  dissociative (conversion)
      disorder 61
  panic disorder 77
  phobic disorders 81
  post-traumatic stress
      disorder 83
  unexplained somatic
      complaints 97
  withdrawal 58
antipsychotics 32–3, 45
  atypical 17
  delirium 49
  dementia 53
  injectable long-acting 45
  side-effects 45–6
  typical 17
anxiety
  adjustment disorder 20
  alcohol misuse 26
  antidepressants 73
  attitude changes 176–7
  common forms 176–7
  exposure 176–7
  management 73, 143
  medication 176–7
  panic disorder 75, 76
  resources 121
  symptoms 176–7
  treatments 176–7
anxiety and depression, chronic
    mixed (F41.2) 19, 39–42, 55
  advice/support to patient and
      family 40–41
  diagnosis 39

anxiety and depression, chronic
    mixed (F41.2)—contd
    differential diagnosis 39–40
    information for patient and
        family 40, 42
    medication 41
    presentation 39
    referral 41
anxiety, generalized (F41.1) 19, 23,
    39, 71–74
    advice/support to patient and
        family 72
    cognitive/behavioural therapy
        (CBT) 73
    diagnosis/differential
        diagnosis 71
    drug use disorders 63
    information for patient and
        family 71, 73–4
    medication 73
    presentation 71
    referral 73
    sleep problems 92
approved social worker (ASW) 141
    assessment under Mental
        Health Act England and
        Wales 103–6, 141
    assessment under Mental
        Health (Northern Ireland)
        Order 109–11, 141
aspirin 53
assertiveness training 143
autism 99
    resources 129

behavioural therapy 143
    post-traumatic stress
        disorder 84
    see also cognitive behavioural
        therapy
benefits resources 135
benzodiazepines 33
    withdrawal 65
    see also diazepam
bereavement (Z63) 19, 28–30
    advice/support to patient and
        family 29
    counselling 29, 30
    depression 28–9
    diagnosis 28
    differential diagnosis 28–9
    information for patient and
        family 29, 30, 121–22

medication 29
    presentation 28
    referral 30
    resources 30, 121–22
    sleep disturbance 29
beta-blockers
    anxiety 73
        performance 81
    post-traumatic stress
        disorder 83
binge eating 67, 69
bipolar disorder (F31) 31–34, 39,
    43, 55
    advice/support to patient and
        family 32
    diagnosis 31
    differential diagnosis 31
    information for patient and
        family 31–32, 34, 122
    medication 32–4
    presentation 31
    referral 34
    resources 34, 122
breathing techniques 143
    relaxation 181
British National Formulary
    (BNF) 4, 8
bulimia 67–70
    resources 127
buprenorphine 66
buproprion 34

carbamazepine 33
care, shared 9
Care Programme Approach
    (CPA) 7
    bipolar disorder 34
    chronic psychotic disorders 46
carers
    needs 7
    resources 122–3
Carer's Recognition and Services
    Act 7
case registers, joint 9
cerebral palsy resources 129
child guidance clinics 142
child psychiatric clinics 142
children
    psychiatric assessment 142
    resources 123, 131–2
chlordiazepoxide 25
chronic fatigue/chronic fatigue
    syndrome 35–8, 178–9

advice/support to
    patient/family 36–7
behavioural strategies 179
depression 37
diagnostic features 35
differential diagnosis 36
information for patient and
    family 36, 37–8
medication 37
physical activity 179
presentation 35
referral 37
treatments 178
triggers 178
chronic tiredness 178–9
citalopram 57
    panic disorder 77
clinical psychologists 140
clinical resources 138
clomipramine 73, 90
cocaine 65
cognitive behavioural
    psychotherapy and exposure 81
cognitive behavioural therapy
    (CBT) 144
    anxiety 73
    bulimia 70
    unexplained somatic
        complaints 97
cognitive therapy 144
    post-traumatic stress
        disorder 84
communication, primary and
    secondary care 8–9
community care workers 141–42
community learning disability
    nurses 142
community mental health
    services 46
    liaison 137
community mental health
    teams 140
community psychiatric
    nurses 138
community resources,
    information 9
compulsive behaviour,
    behavioural therapy 143
compulsory admission
    Mental Health Act England and
        Wales 103–6
    Mental Health (Northern
        Ireland) Order 107–11

Mental Health (Scotland)
    Act 112–9
copyright for diagnostic and
    management summaries 9
counselling 144
    adjustment disorder 20
    alcohol misuse 26
    bereavement 29, 30
    eating disorders 68, 69
    primary care 148
    relationship 85
    resources 123–4
        for professionals 132–3
counsellors 4
cross-cultural applicability 2

day care services 142
debt advice resources 125
delirium (F05) 15, 48–9, 51
    diagnosis 48
    differential diagnosis 48–9
    information, advice and support
        for patient and family 49
    medication 49
    presentation 48
    referral 49
dementia (F00) 50–54, 99
    advice/support to patient and
        family 52–3
    diagnosis 50–1
    differential diagnosis 51
    information for patient and
        family 51–52, 54, 125
    medication 53
    presentation 50
    referral 53
    resources 54, 125
depression (F32) 18, 23, 39, 43, 51,
    55–9, 180–1
    advice/support to patient and
        family 56–7
    alcohol misuse 26
    attitude changing 179
    bereavement 28–9
    bipolar disorder 31, 32, 122
    care training 147
    chronic fatigue/chronic fatigue
        syndrome 37
    diagnosis 55
    differential diagnosis 55–6
    dissociative (conversion)
        disorder 60
    drug use disorders 63

depression (F32)—*contd*
  eating disorders 67
  female sexual disorders 85
  information for patient and
    family 56, 59, 122, 125–6
  learning disability 100
  medication 57–8, 181
  post-traumatic stress
    disorder 83
  presentation 55
  referral 58–9
  resources 59, 122, 125–6
  structured problem-solving
    144–5, 181
  symptoms 180
  treatments 180
  triggers 180
  unexplained somatic complaints
    95, 97
  see also bipolar disorder (F31)
detoxification, alcohol misuse
  25, 26
diagnosis 2
  multi-axial approach 7
diagnostic categories 2
diagnostic summaries
  development 3–4
  dissemination 9
  evidence base 4–5
  local adaptation 9
diazepam 17
  anxiety 73
  bipolar disorder 33
dieticians 142
dissociative (conversion) disorder
  (F44) 20, 60–1
  advice/support for patient and
    family 61
  diagnosis/differential diagnosis
    60
  information for patient and
    family 60, 61
  medication 61
  presentation 60
  referral 61
domestic violence resources 125
dothiepin 57–8
Down's syndrome 99
  resources 129
driving, acute psychotic
  disorders 16
drug use disorders (F11) 39, 40,
  43, 44, 55, 62–6

advice/support to patient and
  family 63–5
depression 59
diagnostic features 62–3
differential diagnosis 63
eating disorders 68, 70
goals 63, 64
harm reduction 63, 64
information for patient and
  family 63, 66, 126–7
medication 65–6
Mental Health (Scotland) Act
  (1984) 113
post-traumatic stress
  disorder 82
presentation 62
referral 66
relapse 65
resources 66, 126–7
withdrawal 62, 65
dyspareunia 86

eating disorders (F50) 67–70
  advice and support for patient
    and family 68–9
  counselling 68, 69
  diagnosis 67
  differential diagnosis 67–8
  information for patient and
    family 68, 70, 127
  medication 69
  presentation 67
  referral 69–70
  resources 70, 127
education, mental health
  147, 148
education welfare officers 142
educational psychologists 142
ejaculation
  premature 89–90
  retarded 90
epilepsy 99, 100
erectile dysfunction 88–9
ethnic minorities, resources 128
evidence base for diagnostic and
  management summaries 4–5
evidence-based mental
  health 139
exposure therapy 81, 143, 175

family therapy 70
fluoxetine 57, 69

general practitioner (GP)
  assessment under Mental Health Act England and Wales (1983) 103–6
  assessment under Mental Health (Northern Ireland) Order (1986) 107–11
  assessment under Mental Health (Scotland) Act (1984) 112–9
graded exposure 143
guidelines, locally adapted 9
gynaecological disorders 85

haloperidol 17, 45
handbook use
  group use 8–9
  individual practitioner 6–8
hearing impairment 99
hepatitis 63
HIV infection 63
homelessness resources 135
Hypericum perforata 41, 57
hyperventilation 143
hypnotic medication 93
hypothyroidism 99

ICD-10 Chapter V 5–6
ICD-10 classification of mental disorders 2, 4
  connections to 5–6
ICD-10 PC 5–6
imipramine 73
  unexplained somatic complaints 97
inborn errors of metabolism 99
insomnia *see* sleep problems (F51)
International Diagnostic and Management Guidelines for Mental Disorders in Primary Care (WHO) 3
internet resources 139
interpersonal therapy 144

key worker
  appointment in psychotic disorders 17, 46
  bipolar disorder 34
Korsakoff syndrome 113

lead poisoning 99
learning disability (F70) 3, 98–102
  advice/support for patient and family 99–100
  co-morbid condition diagnosis 98–9
  community nurses 142
  diagnostic features 98
  differential diagnosis 99
  information for patient and family 99, 101–2
  medication 100
  non-statutory services in Scotland 119
  presentation 98
  referral 100–1
  resources 128–9
  statutory services in Scotland 117–8
  teams 142
  transition plan 100
Lewy-body disease 50, 53
lithium 32, 33
local anaesthetic sprays 90
local services 9
lofexidine 66
lorazepam 17
  bipolar disorder 33

management interventions 2
management plans 3
  partnership with patient 6
management summaries
  development 3–4
  dissemination 9
  evidence base 4–5
  local adaptation 9
mania 31, 32, 122
  see also bipolar disorder (F31)
Maudsley Prescribing Guidelines 18
ME *see* chronic fatigue/chronic fatigue syndrome
medication 7–8
  depression symptoms 56
  key statements 4–5
  recommendations 4, 5
  side-effects 18, 56
memory loss 49–50
mental disorders 103, 113
  Mental Health Act England and Wales (1983) 103
  Mental Health (Northern Ireland) Order (1986) 107, 108
  Mental Health (Scotland) Act (1984) 112, 113
  prevalence 11

mental handicap, Mental Health
(Northern Ireland) Order
(1986) 108
mental health
education 147, 148
evidence-based 139
professionals 140–2
resources 129–31
skills assessment 8
social workers 141
see also community mental
health services
Mental Health Act England and
Wales (1983) 3–4
admission arrangement 105–6
assessment 103–6
arrangements 104
process 104–5
Code of Practice 106
compulsory admission 103
legal issues 16
patients not admitted 106
use 103–4
warrants 103
Mental Health (Northern Ireland)
Order (1986) 107–11
admission arrangement 111
arranging assessment 108
community assessment 107
compulsory admission 107–8,
109–11
follow-up for patient not
admitted 111
hospital assessment 107
information for assessment 109
serious physical harm 107, 108,
110–1
Mental Health Officer (MHO)
113–6, 141
Mental Health (Scotland) Act
(1984) 112–9
assessment 114–5
Code of Practice 116
compulsory admission 113,
115–6
detained patient on leave of
absence 112–3
emergency detention 116
recommendation 112
follow-up care for patients not
admitted 116
information for assessment
113–4

local statutory services 117,
118
non-emergency admission 112
non-statutory services 119
power of entry 112
mental illness
Mental Health Act England and
Wales (1983) 103
Mental Health (Northern
Ireland) Order (1986) 108
Mental Health (Scotland) Act
(1984) 113
resources 129–31
mental impairment
Mental Health Act England and
Wales (1983) 103
Mental Health (Northern
Ireland) Order (1986) 108
Mental Health (Scotland) Act
(1984) 113
mental retardation *see* learning
disability (F70)
methadone 64, 65, 66

narcolepsy 93
neuroleptic malignant syndrome
17
night terrors 93
non-compliance 6
acute psychotic disorders 17
non-statutory organizations,
referral 12
nurse
child guidance/psychiatric
clinics 142
community learning disability
142
community psychiatric 140
primary care 4

obsessional behaviour 143
obsessive compulsive disorder
143
occupational therapists 141, 142
olanzapine 17, 45
opiates 65, 66
orgasmic dysfunction 88

panic disorder (F41.0) 75–8
advice/support for patient and
family 76
diagnosis 75
differential diagnosis 75

graded exposure 143
information for patient and
    family 75–6, 77–8
medication 76–7
presentation 75
resources 77–8, 121
paranoid psychosis, drug-
    induced 113
parents, resources 131–32
parkinsonism 45, 49
paroxetine 57, 73, 80
panic disorder 77
patient groups 4
patient information 136–7
leaflets 9
patients
partners 6
responsibility to help selves 6
support 136–7
phenylketonuria 99
phobic disorders (F40) 79–81
advice/support for patient and
    family 79–81
behavioural therapy 143
diagnosis 79
differential diagnosis 79
graded exposure 143
information for patient and
    family 79, 81
presentation 79
referral 81
resources 81, 121
physical harm
resources 133
serious 107–8, 110–1
physiotherapists 142
play therapists 142
post-traumatic stress disorder
    (F43.1) 19, 71, 82–4
advice/support for patient and
    family 83
depression 83
diagnostic features 82
differential diagnosis 82–3
information for patient and
    family 83, 84
medication 83
presentation 82
referral 84
practice organization 136
primary care
counselling 148
facilitation programme 148

group and mental health skills
    assessment 8
nurses 4
service development 138–9
team
    stress management 137
    working 8–9
see also training
problem-solving, structured 96–7,
    143, 144–5, 179
anxiety 40–1
prostaglandin E$_1$ 89
psychiatrists 140, 142
psychoanalysts 141
psychodynamic therapy 145
psychological therapies 137,
    143–5
psychologists 142
clinical 140
psychopathic disorder 103
psychosexual treatment 88–9
psychotherapists 141
psychotherapy 4–5
analytical 145
anorexia 70
resources 123–5
psychotic disorders, drug use
disorders 63
psychotic disorders, acute (F23)
    15–8, 55
advice 16
diagnostic features 15
differential diagnosis 15–6
family information 16
information for patient and
    carer 16, 44, 46–7
medication 17–8
presentation 15
referral 16–7
relapses 17
resources for patients and
    families 18
support 16
psychotic disorders, chronic
    (F20) 43–7
advice/support for patient and
    carer 44–5
diagnosis 43
differential diagnosis 43–4
medication 45–6
presentation 43
referral 46
public health 2

referral
  criteria 12–3
  information required 12–3
  letters 12
  recommendations 4
relationship problems
  resources 132
relaxation training 40, 143
resources 1–2
  in the community 9
  directory 12
risperidone 17, 45

St. John's wort 41, 57
schizophrenia, resources 133
schools, education services 142
secondary care
  referral 12
  team working 8–9
selective serotonin re-uptake
    inhibitor (SSRI) 90
  alcohol misuse 26
  chronic fatigue/chronic fatigue
    syndrome 37
  panic disorder 77
  post-traumatic stress
    disorder 83
self-harm 133
self-management 145
service provision, gaps 8
sexual desire lack/loss 85–6, 90
sexual disorders
  behavioural therapy 143
  female (F52) 85–7
    diagnosis/differential
      diagnosis 85
    information, advice and
      support for patient and
      partner 85–7
    presentation 85
    referral 87
  male (F52) 88–91
    diagnosis/differential
      diagnosis 88
    information, advice and
      support for patient and
      partner 88–90, 91
    medication 89
    presentation 88
    referral 90
Sheriff, compulsory admission in
    Scotland 115
sildenafil 89

sleep apnoea 92
sleep hygiene training 93
sleep problems (F51) 37, 92–4,
    182–3
  advice/support for family 93
  bereavement 29
  causes 180
  depression 58
  diagnosis/differential diagnosis
    92
  information for patient and
    family 92, 94
  lifestyle change strategies 182
  medication 93, 183
  presentation 92
  referral 93
  slow breathing for relaxation
    181
  symptoms 182
  treatments 182
social care
  services 142
  team working 8–9
social phobia 79–81
Social Services
  carer needs assessment 7
  referral 12
  transition plan for person with
    learning disability 100
social workers
  child guidance/psychiatric
    clinics 142
  mental health 141
  see also approved social worker
    (ASW)
sodium valproate 33
somatic complaints, unexplained
    (F45) 19, 39–40, 56, 60, 95–7,
    184–5
  advice/support to patient and
    family 96–7
  attitude changing 185
  diagnosis 95
  differential diagnosis 95
  information for patient/family
    95–6
  medication 97
  physical activity 185
  presentation 95
  referral 97
  strategies 185
  treatments 184–5
somnambulism 93

speech and language
   therapists 142
SSRI *see* selective serotonin re-
   uptake inhibitor (SSRI)
street drugs, co-morbid use 17
stress
   acute reaction 19–21
   anxiety 40
   erectile dysfunction 88–9
   management 143
      for primary-care team 137
   parental 131–2
   reduction 71, 72
   resources for professionals
      132–3
   sleep problems 92
   unexplained somatic complaints
      95, 96
stressful events 20
substance abuse, liaison with
   services 137
suicidal feelings, resources 134
suicide risk 29, 32, 41, 56, 70
   post-traumatic stress
      disorder 83
support workers 141–2

team working 8–9
thiamine in alcohol misuse 24, 25

tiredness, chronic *see* chronic
   fatigue/chronic fatigue syndrome
training 146–51
   courses 147–8
   information 146–7
   primary care 8
   resources for trainers 148–51
   skills-based 148–51
trauma, resources 134
tricyclic antidepressants 57–8
   chronic fatigue/chronic fatigue
      syndrome 37
   panic disorder 77
   post-traumatic stress disorder 83
   unexplained somatic
      complaints 97

vaginismus 86
valerian 93
vascular dementia 50, 53
venlafaxine 73
victim support resources 134
visual impairment 99
voluntary organizations, referral 12

unexplained somatic complaints
   184–5

welfare resources 135